T0347924

PREFACE

Educating Individuals With Severe Disabilities

Fred P. Orelove and Stacy K. Dymond
Guest Editors

It is difficult to think of many professional disciplines that grew out of court decisions and federal legislation. However, as we observe in our article in this issue, the field of teaching individuals with severe disabilities is one of them. Children with severe disabilities, of course, have been with us since recorded time. Although public schools provided special education services to children with milder learning and behavioral challenges, few took it on themselves to serve the child with severe or profound mental retardation, deafness and blindness, or multiple disabilities. Most of those children who did receive educational services benefitted from the hard work of parents and advocates who used church basements and other makeshift locales. It took the passage of Pub. L. 94–142 in 1975—which built on several key successful lawsuits—to force states to educate all children.

Many of those children stumped the educational system. There were few university teacher preparation programs to work with children with severe disabilities. No curricula or organized teaching methods existed. Moreover, more than a few administrators questioned whether such children "belonged" in public schools or if they were capable of learning.

Much has changed in the past quarter century. The field has grown and matured. There are active research and training programs in every state, countless textbooks and journal articles on curriculum and instructional techniques, a professional association, and—of primary importance—a general acceptance that all means all.

As with any profession that has reached maturity, it is easy to feel pride in all that has been accomplished. Maturity, however, should not suggest failure to grow. On the contrary, we have much to learn about how best to meet the varied and complex needs of students with severe disabilities. Moreover, given the enhanced focus during the past decade on inclusive education, it has been easy to forget that learners with profound mental retardation or multiple disabilities continue to present us with significant teaching challenges.

This issue of *Exceptionality* provides a wonderful opportunity to step back and to discover—or rediscover, in some instances—some of what many people working in this field find so challenging, important, and rewarding. The first article, by Dymond and Orelove, takes a fresh look at the questions surrounding effective curriculum for learners with severe disabilities in a new era of the Individuals With Disabilities Education Act, alternate assessment, and inclusive education. The article ends with recommendations for needed research.

The next three articles focus on learners with the most significant disabilities. Logan and Gast review the literature on preference assessment and reinforcer testing, with special attention to individuals with profound multiple disabilities. These authors provide detailed instructions for conducting preference assessment with this population. Smith, Gast, Logan, and Jacobs describe a process for customizing instruction for this same group of learners. The process is designed around collaborative teamwork and problem solving, with considerable emphasis on handling and positioning techniques, and instructional adaptations and materials. Taking a more specialized instructional focus, Downing describes a rationale for teaching communication skills, particularly within a team approach. She emphasizes the importance of communication partners taking responsibility for supporting communicative interactions.

The fifth article, by Lohrmann-O'Rourke and Gomez, describes a detailed process for integrating preference assessment within the transition process for meaningful school-to-life outcomes. The authors also delve into special considerations and offer ideas for future research.

We hope this issue will whet your appetite for conducting further research and demonstration studies in the field of severe disabilities.

What Constitutes Effective Curricula for Students With Severe Disabilities?

Stacy K. Dymond

School of Education
Virginia Commonwealth University

Fred P. Orelove

Virginia Institute for Developmental Disabilities
Virginia Commonwealth University

During the last quarter century, the definition of *effective curriculum* for students with severe disabilities has changed dramatically. This article reviews the development of curriculum practices for students with severe disabilities and examines 3 components of the 1997 Individuals With Disabilities Education Act (IDEA) that have the potential to significantly impact curriculum design. These components include (a) IDEA's emphasis on preparing students for employment and independent living, (b) mandates for student access to the general curriculum, and (c) students with disabilities in state- and district-wide assessments. The benefits and challenges of implementing these changes are explored in relation to the current literature on effective curriculum models. Future research questions for evaluating the impact of IDEA's framework on student outcomes are presented.

The question "What shall we teach and why shall we teach that?" serves as the foundation for virtually any educational endeavor. The modern discipline of teaching students with severe disabilities is now 25 years old, having been born with the passage of Pub. L. 94–142, The Education for All Handicapped Children Act of 1975, which, of course, is now known as the Individuals With Disabilities Education Act (IDEA; 1997). Twenty-five years is old enough to have a history of its own and young enough for us to remember all of it.

Requests for reprints may be sent to Stacy K. Dymond, Department of Special Education, College of Education, 288 Education Building, 1310 South 6th Street, Champaign, IL 61820.

The earliest attempts at curriculum design for learners with severe disabilities were based on those students' behavioral characteristics or "developmental levels." The theory was that children who performed on developmental tests at a very young age should be taught skills that were typically performed by very young children. Teaching those skills in a "normal," predictable sequence was done to remediate delays and prevent further delays and disabilities (Rainforth & York-Barr, 1997).

However, it became clear by the late 1970s that a developmental approach had many drawbacks. In what is viewed as a classic article in the field, Brown, Nietupski, and Hamre-Nietupski (1976) laid the groundwork for the next generation of curriculum and instructional design. Their concept of the "criterion of ultimate functioning" suggested that individuals with severe disabilities ultimately would be expected to be productive members of their communities. Therefore, services must be longitudinal and continuous, rather than short term or episodic, and they must be conducted in regular community-based public schools. Moreover, tasks, materials, and settings should be as close to natural as possible.

The criterion of ultimate functioning gave rise to the functional curriculum approach that dominated the 1980s. The concept of *functional* referred to activities performed by people without disabilities, typically in natural (or functional) settings. The other main practice is that tasks and materials were *age appropriate*—that is, relevant to the student's chronological age, rather than developmental age as determined by a test.

The functional approach to curriculum was a vast improvement over earlier models, yet the content of functional curricula was largely idiosyncratic, with no established criteria for determining what was functional or relevant for an individual student (Rainforth & York-Barr, 1997). In Brown et al. (1979), the next generation of curriculum design was based on the environments in which a specific student currently performed, or was expected to perform, and those activities and skills that were most relevant for that student in those environments. In this environmental or ecological approach, the specific content evolved continually as the student's needs, goals, and opportunities changed (Falvey, 1989; Ford et al., 1989).

Over the past decade, a sea change has been underway. Inclusive education has changed the way many educators think about how and what to teach—indeed, the very purpose of education. As the field has moved increasingly toward educating students with severe disabilities in the general education classroom, questions about appropriate curriculum content have become increasingly evident. In our experience, there are some instances where inclusion appears to have become the curriculum. That is, students participate in the same activities as their peers without disabilities, regardless of whether the curriculum enables them to achieve competence across a variety of academic and functional skill areas. Membership in the classroom is seen as the goal, and inclusion is justified based on the opportunities it provides for learning social and communication skills. On the opposite end of the continuum, curriculum in an inclusive classroom sometimes has been modeled on a miniature version of a self-contained classroom, where students work separate from their peers on activities that are different and unrelated to the general education curriculum. The student is physically present but is not an equally participating member of the classroom. Clearly, neither form of inclusion offers an ideal curriculum for most students with severe disabilities.

During the past decade, published research on curriculum design has decreased substantially (Nietupski, Hamre-Nietupski, Curtin, & Shrikanth, 1997). In addition, the focus of this research has shifted from an emphasis on functional skills to one that simultaneously includes attention to interactions with students without disabilities and inclusion. In an analysis of the literature between 1976 and 1995, Nietupski et al. found a 32% decrease in articles addressing functional skills and a 231% increase in articles focusing on interactions and inclusion. Billingsley (1997) noted a 53% decrease in functional skills articles in ERIC between 1985–1989 and 1991–1995, and a 71% decrease in functional skills articles published in JASH between 1984–1988 and 1993–1997. Our own examination of the literature between 1996 and May 2000 indicates a similar trend. Functional skills, which once were widely accepted as the basis for curriculum development, have received limited attention as the field has moved to a more inclusive service delivery model.

The past decade has resulted in a plethora of research articles demonstrating the social benefits of inclusion for students with severe disabilities and their peers without disabilities. Relatively limited attention has been given to defining and evaluating other forms of curriculum content. Although student outcomes in the areas of academics and functional skills have been chronicled on a limited basis in the literature, most of these studies are based on stakeholder perceptions as opposed to empirical data (Dymond, 2000). As a result, one must question the extent to which conclusions can be drawn about student outcomes in these areas.

The question "What constitutes an effective curriculum for students with severe disabilities?" remains an elusive topic, particularly for students served in inclusive classrooms. Although validated strategies for developing curriculum for inclusive settings exist (see Giangreco, Cloninger, Dennis, & Edelman, 1993; Giangreco, Edelman, Dennis, & Cloninger, 1995), the research literature provides limited documentation regarding effective curriculum strategies that lead to student outcomes in the areas of academics and functional skills acquisition. The resurgence of discussion regarding the nature of curriculum and the future role of functional skills (see Billingsley & Albertson, 1999; Browder, 1997; Nietupski et al., 1997) suggests that researchers and practitioners would do well to balance their attention equally on academic, functional, and social skills, keeping in mind that the relative emphasis placed on each content area depends on the needs of the individual child.

The remainder of this article explores the struggle to develop effective curriculum for students with severe disabilities in the next quarter century. Our review and discussion are guided by four questions:

1. What guidance does IDEA (1997) offer on curriculum design?
2. To what degree does the literature define strategies for implementing the curriculum framework set forth in IDEA?
3. What challenges exist for implementing the curriculum elements of IDEA?
4. What future research questions must be addressed to extend our understanding of effective education for students with severe disabilities?

THE IMPACT OF IDEA ON CURRICULUM DEVELOPMENT

The inclusive school movement has challenged the field to think differently about the curriculum focus for students with severe disabilities. At the same time, recent changes to

IDEA (1997) have and will continue to have a direct impact on the scope of curriculum offered to students. These changes have the potential to significantly improve the quality of each student's education. At the same time, they present unique challenges to the field that are unlike any faced before.

We have selected three components of IDEA (1997) that we believe have the most direct impact on the future of curriculum development for students with severe disabilities. These include the described purpose of IDEA, mandates for student access to the general curriculum, and the inclusion of students with disabilities in state accountability systems. This section defines these changes, explores their relation to the current literature pertaining to effective curriculum models, and identifies the challenges that exist.

The Purpose of IDEA

Although one of the express purposes of IDEA (1997) always has been to ensure a free and appropriate education for all children with disabilities, these amendments articulate for the first time that special education and related services should prepare students for employment and independent living (34 C.F.R. § 300.1 (a)). The law makes clear that the educational supports and services provided for students with disabilities should lead to clear and measurable outcomes in adulthood. This purpose is consistent with the educational goals held for all students, regardless of disability.

Implementation of a functional curriculum that includes age-appropriate, community-referenced, and community-based instruction has been linked to student acquisition of desired postschool outcomes (Wehman, Hess, & Kregel, 1996). At the same time, education in inclusive school classrooms has yielded promising evidence of student achievement in a variety of curriculum areas (see Giangreco, Dennis, Cloninger, Edelman, & Schattman, 1993; Ryndak, Downing, Jacqueline, & Morrison, 1995). With the movement toward inclusive schooling, it remains unclear how much time should be devoted to instruction in the school and community, under what circumstances and at what ages community-based instruction may be appropriate, and whether community-based instruction is compatible with an inclusive approach to education.

Some have argued that functional skills, including independent living and vocational skills, should be taught within the context of naturally occurring routines that occur in general education classrooms and the school environment (Schuh, Tashie, Lamb, Bang, & Jorgensen, 1998; Tashie, Jorgensen, Shapiro-Barnard, Martin, & Schuh, 1996). Students with disabilities who participate in community-based instruction do not have access to their peers without disabilities who are in school, and they miss out on opportunities for learning the academic and social skills that are critical for adulthood. It has been suggested that instruction in the community should occur after school or on weekends (the time when peers would normally be in the community) or during ages 19–21 when inclusion in the high school curriculum would not be age appropriate (Fisher & Sax, 1999; Schuh et al., 1998; Tashie et al., 1996).

Proponents of a curriculum that supports school and community inclusion (i.e., instruction in the general education classroom, other school environments, and the community) have advocated for balancing functional skills instruction across multiple environments, depending on the needs of the student (Agran, Snow, & Swaner, 1999;

Dymond, 1997; McDonnell, 1997). Although numerous opportunities abound for teaching functional skills in school settings (i.e., community-referenced instruction), some skills simply cannot be taught at school. In other instances, teaching in the community may be necessary to ensure that students generalize skills learned in school to other applicable environments. A recent survey of middle and high school teachers suggests that inclusive education and community-based instruction are both instrumental in teaching students social skills and preparing them for postschool outcomes (Agran et al., 1999).

Consensus exists regarding the need for functional skills and community experiences that will enable students to achieve desired postschool outcomes. Methods for achieving these outcomes (i.e., through inclusive education or through a combination of inclusive school and community instruction) have produced considerable discussion. Several additional points warrant attention as questions about the interface between inclusive education and community-based instruction are examined.

First, public school education is an entitlement service. That is, under IDEA (1997), all students qualify for educational services until age 21. There are no exceptions. Unlike the public school system, when students transition to adulthood, disability-related services and programs are based on a system of eligibility. Some young adults qualify for services, and some do not. Although many adult service agencies do exemplary work in supporting individuals in their communities, our discussions with teachers suggest that, all too often, individuals with severe disabilities are put on long waiting lists for services or targeted for programs that support segregated activities. Employment is often not considered unless it is in a sheltered workshop. If we provide students with inclusive opportunities during their school years, we must ensure that those opportunities continue to be available during adulthood. Focusing on community skills and employment at age 19, when inclusion in the high school is no longer appropriate, may not provide adequate time for students with the most severe disabilities to acquire the skills and supports needed for inclusion in their community. Similar to the options available to all high school students, youths with severe disabilities should be afforded the opportunity to develop work and independent living skills in the community, as appropriate to their needs, preferences, and future goals.

Second, perhaps it is time to redefine our concept of community-based instruction in a way that incorporates our shared understanding of inclusion. McDonnell (1997) posited that all students can benefit from instruction in the community. For students without disabilities, community-based instruction allows application of concepts learned in the classroom to real-life situations. For students with severe disabilities, the community offers opportunities to generalize skills across settings and to learn new skills that would otherwise be taught through simulated instruction at school. Examples exist for involving students with and without disabilities in the community through community-based instruction (see Beck, Broers, Hogue, Shipstead, & Knowlton, 1994; Dymond, 1997), service learning activities (see Gent & Gurecka, 1998), and integrated research teams (see "Team Your Students," 1996). Inclusive education need not occur only within the confines of the school building.

Finally, in considering the age at which students receive community-based instruction, recent discussion has advocated its use for post-high school programs and questioned its appropriateness during high school. We would like to suggest that in keeping with the individualized nature of special education, we refrain from the tendency to assign ages to this form of instruction. One can imagine an elementary school student who, because of the severity of his behavior, did not have access to the community outside of school hours because of parent concerns for safety. An Individual Education Program (IEP) team might assess the function of the behavior and develop an intervention plan that includes the home, school, and community settings. The school then might work collaboratively with the parents to teach new behaviors in the community during school hours so that the student's inclusion could be expanded beyond the 6 hr that were spent in school. By narrowly defining *inclusion* as specific to the school, might we not inadvertently create *exclusion* for some students who require direct community instruction to participate outside of school hours?

Access to the General Curriculum

The 1997 amendments to IDEA communicate a clear expectation that students with disabilities will participate in the general curriculum. The regulations define the general curriculum as the "same curriculum as for nondisabled students" (34 C.F.R. § 300.347 (a)(1)(i)). IEP goals should be designed to meet the child's needs that result from the child's disability and reflect goals that enable him or her to (a) make progress in the general curriculum and (b) meet other educational needs (34 C.F.R. § 300.347 (a)(2)). The law recognizes the importance of ensuring that students with disabilities have the opportunity to achieve the same high standards as their peers without disabilities. At the same time, it acknowledges that access to the general curriculum should not circumvent attention to other goals that may be equally important in promoting desirable student outcomes.

There appears to be a growing trend toward emphasizing an academic curriculum (one of the most prominent components of the general curriculum) for students with severe disabilities in inclusive elementary school classrooms. Alhough limited, preliminary data indicate that students with severe disabilities served in a full inclusion model have more academic objectives and fewer functional skills objectives than students in self-contained classrooms (Hunt, Farron-Davis, Beckstead, Curtis, & Goetz, 1994) and spend significantly more time engaged in academic instruction than any other type of curriculum activity (Logan & Malone, 1998a, 1998b). In addition, students who spend their day in both general and special education classrooms receive instruction primarily on academic content in the general education classroom, whereas in the special education classroom the curriculum is balanced between academic and functional skills (Helmstetter, Curry, Brennan, & Sampson-Saul, 1998).

These studies raise several questions regarding the manner in which students gain access to the general curriculum and the relative importance placed on academics in comparison to other goal areas (i.e., functional skills). It is interesting to note that the findings (Helmstetter et al., 1998; Hunt et al., 1994; Logan & Malone, 1998a, 1998b) seem to suggest that there may be a relation between the environment in which a student is educated and the emphasis that is placed on the general curriculum. What is not clear is whether decisions about curriculum are based on the student's placement in the general education classroom or their individual needs for learning. That is, is an academic curriculum focus chosen for a child because it assists with their inclusion in the general education classroom or because it meets their individual needs for learning? We hope that consideration is given to both factors.

With increased emphasis placed on ensuring access to the general curriculum, there is a need to further define methods that allow students to gain access to the general curriculum in ways that maximize their inclusion with same-age peers and enable achievement of priority IEP goals. Although numerous approaches exist for effectively adapting the general curriculum (e.g., see Udvari-Solner, 1997), research on specialized instructional strategies for students with severe disabilities has failed to keep pace with changes in the field's thinking about curriculum. In particular, the principles of systematic instruction (e.g., prompting strategies, generalization, maintenance, and embedding skills) have received limited attention in recent years, particularly as to if and how they relate to (a) teaching the general curriculum and (b) use in inclusive classrooms.

Given the lack of attention to specialized strategies for educating students with severe disabilities, we believe there exists the potential for redefining the general curriculum according to some of the standards and practices of general education. In special education terminology, that includes judging access to the general curriculum based on a student's developmental level, focusing on drill and practice activities that include massed trials, and viewing students as "not ready" for certain activities because they lack prerequisite skills. Our challenge lies in merging our knowledge of effective instructional strategies for students with severe disabilities within the context of a classroom environment that inadvertently may promote a deficit model.

Although our discussion thus far has focused on how students access the general curriculum in inclusive classrooms, we would be remiss if we did not acknowledge the demands that are present in noninclusive classrooms. The law does not specify how or where students access the general curriculum (e.g., general education classroom or special education classroom). Equally important, it does not specify who is eligible to teach the general curriculum. As a result, it remains questionable whether student opportunities to pursue the general curriculum will differ based on placement. It also begs the question, "Is access to the general curriculum truly access to the same curriculum when it is taught in a self-contained classroom?" Likewise, do special education teachers have sufficient content expertise (not just specialized strategies) to teach the general curriculum? One need only look at the arguments contained in *Brown v. Board of Education* (1954) to be reminded that separate is not necessarily equal.

One final challenge bears mentioning. Regardless of where students with severe disabilities receive their education, the requirement of access to the general curriculum will continue to create discussion within the field regarding how best to balance attention between academic and functional skills instruction. As more students with severe disabilities are served in the general education classroom, decisions about curriculum focus will need to take into consideration both the student's individual needs and methods for enhancing inclusion.

The concept of the criterion of ultimate functioning (Brown et al., 1976) still seems relevant as we consider how best to educate learners with severe disabilities. This concept submits that students should pursue skills that are commensurate with their age and their needs for participation in current and future environments. Focusing on academic instruction in the general education classroom would be appropriate according to this premise because it enables students to participate in current, age-appropriate environments where the skills are needed. Issues arise when one simultaneously applies the test of functionality. That is, can the academic skill needed in the general education classroom be taught in a manner that is functional (i.e., meaningful) for the student? Similarly, at what point does instruction on a particular academic skill become nonfunctional and unnecessary in helping a student prepare for future environments?

At issue, in part, is whether the concepts of access to the general curriculum and functional skills are mutually exclusive ideologies. Some have questioned whether students who are pursuing primarily a functional skills curriculum can have their needs met appropriately in the general education classroom (Logan & Malone, 1998b). At the same time, there are calls from those in general education for tying factual knowledge to real-life applications for all students (Brady, 2000). The challenge continues to be how to make the curriculum functional and meaningful for all students, regardless of ability, and regardless of where their education is provided.

Participation in State and District Assessments

Perhaps the most important component of IDEA (1997) that will affect curriculum is the requirement for students to participate in state- and district-wide assessment programs. Under IDEA, students with disabilities may be included in a state's assessment program by participating in the general assessment, the general assessment with accommodations, or the alternate assessment (34 C.F.R. 300.138). To the greatest extent possible, states are expected to develop a system of alternate assessment that complements the state's general assessment. This assessment is designed for a relatively small percentage of students (34 C.F.R. Attachment 1, p. 12564) who are unable to participate in the general assessment, with or without accommodations. It is expected that most students with severe disabilities (i.e., severe and profound cognitive disabilities) will participate in the alternate assessment.

Regardless of where one stands on the issue of state standards and accountability systems, the alternate assessment process has the potential to dramatically improve the quality of educational supports and services for students who traditionally have been excluded from statewide assessment programs. Some of the benefits anticipated from an inclusive assessment system (Dymond & Daniel, 1999; Elliott, Ysseldyke, Thurlow, & Erickson, 1998; National Center on Educational Outcomes, 1996; Ysseldyke & Olsen, 1999) are that

1. All students will participate in programs that include high expectations.
2. Standards will provide a clear framework to guide schools in the development of appropriate curriculum.
3. Communities will be more aware of the progress of all children, because reports of student achievement on both the general and alternate assessment must be reported publicly.
4. Future decisions about funding, policies, programs, and staff development will be based on data obtained regarding the progress of all students, including students with the most severe disabilities.

Despite the many benefits of including all students in statewide accountability systems, the impact of state standards on curriculum development for students with severe disabilities remains to be seen. Preliminary evidence (Kleinert, Kennedy, & Kearns, 1999) suggests that teachers in one state (Kentucky) believe their alternate assessment process has improved instructional programming for students with severe disabilities and enhanced outcomes in the area of communication. As states continue to wrestle with defining appropriate standards and developing valid and reliable methods for measuring student progress on the standards, several points warrant consideration.

Standards, by nature, are designed to provide a framework from which curriculum is developed. The current literature on severe disabilities supports the development of a curriculum that is based on each student's individual needs and preferences, ensures access to the general curriculum, addresses functional skills, and develops social competence (see previous discussion). To the greatest extent possible, this curriculum should be pursued in inclusive school and community settings alongside peers without disabilities, and should lead to desired postschool outcomes in the areas of employment and independent living.

Defining standards that encompass these broad areas is a daunting task, and states have taken different approaches to accomplishing this feat. Since IDEA (1997), the National Center on Educational Outcomes (2000) has monitored the progress of states in developing their systems of alternate assessment. Findings from their Alternate Assessment Cyber Survey as of March 2000 indicate that of the 42 states that have determined the nature of their standards for the alternate assessment, 21 expect to have standards that are a subset of those applied to general education, and 8 will have standards that are identical to those applied to general education. In total, 69% of the states have or will develop an alternate assessment based solely on the standards for the general assessment. Only 13 states (31%) have chosen to either include the standards applied to general education with some additions ($n = 4$) or develop different standards that do not include standards from the general assessment ($n = 9$).

In those states where the standards for the general assessment have been adopted in part or in whole as the sole standards for the alternate assessment, it seems pertinent to question the degree to which those standards initially were formulated to address the educational expectations of all children. If the standards truly were developed to accommodate the diversity of the population, they should result in a curriculum framework for students with severe disabilities that addresses the content areas and instructional practices advocated in the literature. Alternatively, if a state's standards were not developed with all children in mind, it is possible that they may not be broad enough to encompass the full range of curricula needed by students with severe disabilities.

Although IDEA (1997) recognizes the importance of the general curriculum for students with disabilities, it also supports the need for some students to pursue other goals that are not related to the general curriculum. In states where the general curriculum focuses on high academic standards, how do we ensure that schools are held accountable for teaching skills outside the realm of academics? Likewise, if the standards on which the general curriculum is based were not developed with all students in mind, is it possible that students will not have access to certain types of curriculum experiences in the future because they are not addressed on the alternate assessment? The suggestion that what gets tested is what gets taught (Burgess & Kennedy, 1998) is a frightening possibility, especially if what gets tested is not representative of the student's individualized needs or the practices included in the research literature.

Several have questioned whether the standards for the general curriculum are appropriate for students participating in the alternate assessment and submitted that additional standards may be necessary to simultaneously address functional skills (Kleinert & Kearns, 1999; Ysseldyke & Olsen, 1999). Some states that have chosen to adopt all or part of their standards for the general assessment have identified "access skills" (e.g., motor, social, communication) that enable students to pursue functional skills while simultaneously participating in the general curriculum. Others have identified "critical functions" of the state standards (i.e., the functional context for using the skill) and based the assessment process on student performance of the critical functions (Mid-South Regional Resource Center, 1998). Recognizing access skills and critical functions broadens the state standards and allows students to pursue both functional and academic skills as they relate to the general curriculum. Whether the general curriculum, as defined by the state standards, is sufficiently comprehensive for students with severe disabilities to pursue functional skills in meaningful ways remains to be seen.

Perhaps the overall challenge that exists is that of determining how to balance the development of individualized goals and objectives for students with the need to simultaneously address state standards. Although the IEP process traditionally has served as the accountability system for students with disabilities, participation in statewide testing systems will further extend accountability and the measures that are employed to determine its presence. Where the results of the alternate assessment are utilized to determine rewards and sanctions for students and schools (i.e., high-stakes testing), it is possible that IEP teams may find it necessary to write IEPs based on the state standards rather than the student's individualized needs and preferences. Maintaining a balance between standards and the integrity of the IEP process may present significant challenges in the coming years.

EVALUATION OF CURRICULUM EFFORTS

The research literature has provided limited direction in recent years regarding curricula for students with severe disabilities, in part because efforts to identify effective strategies for including students in general education classrooms have taken precedence. In some instances, it appears that the curriculum components advocated are in direct competition with one another. IDEA's (1997) emphasis on postschool outcomes, access to the general curriculum, and participation in statewide accountability systems has the potential to have a significant impact on the type of curriculum pursued by students with severe disabilities. It is important that future research efforts evaluate the effectiveness of new and existing curriculum models to determine the impact of IDEA's framework on student outcomes. We believe there are six core areas that deserve attention.

Methods for Addressing Functional Skills in Inclusive Settings

Research has demonstrated that instruction in functional skills helps students to achieve postschool outcomes. Models are needed that delineate how students can pursue functional skills in the general education classroom while addressing the general curriculum.

Methods for Making Instruction in the Community Inclusive

Examples exist to illustrate the inclusion of students with and without disabilities in community-based instruction. Curriculum models that extend the concept of inclusive education into the community should be explored further to identify effective strategies for structuring community experiences and to evaluate the effectiveness of such models on student achievement.

Curriculum Emphasis in Inclusive Classrooms

Preliminary research suggests that students with severe disabilities spend more time learning academics in the general education classroom than students in other settings. Additional study is warranted to explore the percentage of time students spend in academic, functional, and social skills instruction in inclusive settings; how decisions are made about the curriculum's focus; and student progress across skill areas.

Postschool Outcomes

Acquisition of functional skills helps students with severe disabilities achieve desirable postschool outcomes. Additional research would help define the relation among curriculum emphasis (i.e., the relative emphasis placed on academics, functional skills, and the development of social relationships), the instructional setting (e.g., general education classroom, special education classroom, community), and various other postschool outcomes.

Access to the General Curriculum and Student Progress

IDEA (1997) does not specify the physical location where students must gain access to the general curriculum or the qualifications needed by teachers who provide instruction on the general curriculum. These variables must be examined to determine their impact on student progress in the general curriculum and interpretations regarding how the curriculum is defined and implemented.

Impact of State Standards on Curriculum Design

Given the number of states that are developing systems of alternate assessment based solely on their standards for the general education curriculum, it will be important to analyze the impact that the standards have on the curriculum focus for students with severe disabilities. In particular, one might explore the relation between student achievement on the standards to postschool outcomes and whether differences exist in curriculum focus among states based on the standards chosen.

The field has come a long way since the 1970s, when "cookie-cutter" curricula demanded that all learners be taught the same skills in essentially the same way. Now, in the 21st century, it is good to remind ourselves that the intent of the original federal legislation, Pub. L. 94–142, was to provide each child with an appropriate, individualized education. Prior to the law's enactment by Congress, Senator Jennings Randolph (WV; cited in Newman & Piazza, 1978) stated that

> Individual attention is one of the benefits of a good education in institutions of learning for all people of the United States .... Throughout this country, our schools, colleges, and universities long have stressed the need for individual attention to students. It is the heart of our educational process and it has stood the test of time. (p. 202)

REFERENCES

Agran, M., Snow, K., & Swaner, J. (1999). A survey of secondary level teachers' opinions on community-based instruction and inclusive education. *The Journal of the Association for Persons With Severe Handicaps, 24*, 58–62.

Beck, J., Broers, J., Hogue, E., Shipstead, J., & Knowlton, E. (1994). Strategies for functional community-based instruction and inclusion for children with mental retardation. *Teaching Exceptional Children, 26*(2), 44–48.

Billingsley, F. F. (1997, December). The problem and the place of functional skills in inclusive settings. In G. Singer (Chair), *The role of functional skills and behavioral instructional methods in inclusive education*. Symposium conducted at the annual meeting of TASH, Boston.

Billingsley, F. F., & Albertson, L. R. (1999). Finding a future for functional skills. *The Journal of the Association for Persons With Severe Handicaps, 24*, 298–302.

Brady, M. (2000). The standards juggernaut. *Kappan, 81*, 648–651.

Browder, D. M. (1997). Educating students with severe disabilities: Enhancing the conversation between research and practice. *The Journal of Special Education, 31*, 137–144.

Brown v. Board of Education, 347 U.S. 483 (1954).

Brown, L., Branston-McLean, M. B., Baumgart, D., Vincent, L., Falvey, M., & Schroeder, J. (1979). Using the characteristics of current and future least restrictive environments in the development of curricular content for severely handicapped students. *AAESPH Review, 4*, 407–424.

Brown, L., Nietupski, J., & Hamre-Nietupski, S. (1976). Criterion of ultimate functioning. In M. Thomas (Ed.), *Hey don't forget about me!* (pp. 2–15). Reston, VA: Council of Exceptional Children.

Burgess, P., & Kennedy, S. (1998). *What gets tested, gets taught who gets tested, gets taught: Curriculum framework development process*. Lexington, KY: Mid-South Regional Resource Center.

Dymond, S. K. (1997). Community living. In P. Wehman & J. Kregel (Eds.), *Functional curriculum for elementary, middle, and secondary-age students with special needs* (pp. 197–226). Austin, TX: PRO-ED.

Dymond, S. K. (2000). *The effectiveness of a participatory research approach to evaluating an inclusive school program*. Unpublished doctoral dissertation, School of Education, Virginia Commonwealth University, Richmond.

Dymond, S. K., & Daniel, L. (1999). *Performance indicators and delivery practices for the alternate assessment process*. Richmond: Virginia Department of Education.

Elliott, J., Ysseldyke, J., Thurlow, M., & Erickson, R. (1998). What about assessment and accountability? Practical implications for educators. *Teaching Exceptional Children, 31*(2), 20–27.

Falvey, M. A. (1989). *Community-based curriculum: Instructional strategies for students with severe handicaps* (2nd ed.). Baltimore: Brookes.

Fisher, D., & Sax, C. (1999). Noticing differences between secondary and postsecondary education: Extending Agran, Snow, and Swaner's discussion. *The Journal of the Association for Persons With Severe Handicaps, 24,* 303–305.

Ford, A., Schnorr, R., Meyer, L., Davern, L., Black, J., & Dempsey, P. (Eds.). (1989). *The Syracuse community-referenced curriculum guide for students with moderate and severe disabilities.* Baltimore: Brookes.

Gent, P. J., & Gurecka, L. E. (1998). Service learning: A creative strategy for inclusive classrooms. *The Journal of the Association for Persons With Severe Handicaps, 23,* 261–271.

Giangreco, M. F., Cloninger, C. J., Dennis, R. E., & Edelman, S. W. (1993). National expert validation of COACH: Congruence with exemplary practice and suggestions for improvement. *The Journal of the Association for Persons With Severe Handicaps, 18,* 109–120.

Giangreco, M. F., Dennis, R., Cloninger, C., Edelman, S., & Schattman, R. (1993). "I've counted Jon": Transformational experiences of teachers educating students with disabilities. *Exceptional Children, 59,* 359–372.

Giangreco, M. F., Edelman, S. W., Dennis, R. E., & Cloninger, C. J. (1995). Use and impact of COACH with students who are deaf–blind. *The Journal of the Association for Persons With Severe Handicaps, 20,* 121–135.

Helmstetter, E., Curry, C. A., Brennan, M., & Sampson-Saul, M. (1998). Comparison of general and special education classrooms of students with severe disabilities. *Education and Training in Mental Retardation and Developmental Disabilities, 33,* 216–227.

Hunt, P., Farron-Davis, F., Beckstead, S., Curtis, D., & Goetz, L. (1994). Evaluating the effects of placement of students with severe disabilities in general education versus special classes. *The Journal of the Association for Persons With Severe Handicaps, 19,* 200–214.

Individuals With Disabilities Education Act Amendments of 1997, 20 U.S.C. § 1400 *et seq.* (1997).

Kleinert, H. L., & Kearns, J. F. (1999). A validation study of the performance indicators and learner outcomes of Kentucky's alternate assessment for students with significant disabilities. *The Journal of the Association for Persons With Severe Handicaps, 24,* 100–110.

Kleinert, H. L., Kennedy, S., & Kearns, J. (1999). The impact of alternate assessments: A statewide teacher survey. *The Journal of Special Education, 33,* 93–102.

Logan, K. R., & Malone, D. M. (1998a). Comparing instructional contexts of students with and without severe disabilities in general education classrooms. *Exceptional Children, 64,* 343–358.

Logan, K. R., & Malone, D. M. (1998b). Instructional contexts for students with moderate, severe, and profound intellectual disabilities in general education elementary classrooms. *Education and Training in Mental Retardation and Developmental Disabilities, 33,* 62–75.

McDonnell, J. (1997, February). Participation in content-area classes and community-based instruction in secondary schools: Isn't it about achieving a balance? *TASH Newsletter, 23*(2), 23–24, 29.

Mid-South Regional Resource Center. (1998). *Alternate assessment issues and practices.* Lexington, KY: Author.

National Center on Educational Outcomes. (1996). *Alternate assessments for students with disabilities.* Minneapolis: Author.

National Center on Educational Outcomes. (2000, March). *NCEO survey on state practices in alternate assessment.* Minneapolis: Author. Retrieved March 2000 from the World Wide Web: http://www.umn.edu/nceo/AltSurvey/statistics.asp

Newman, I., & Piazza, R. (Eds.). (1978). *Readings in severely and profoundly handicapped education.* Guilford, CT: Special Learning Corporation.

Nietupski, J., Hamre-Nietupski, S., Curtin, S., & Shrikanth, K. (1997). A review of curricular research in severe disabilities from 1976 to 1995 in six selected journals. *The Journal of Special Education, 31,* 36–55.

Rainforth, B., & York-Barr, J. (1997). *Collaborative teams for students with severe disabilities* (2nd ed.). Baltimore: Brookes.

Ryndak, D. L., Downing, J. E., Jacqueline, L. R., & Morrison, A. P. (1995). Parents' perceptions after inclusion of their children with moderate or severe disabilities. *The Journal of the Association for Persons With Severe Handicaps, 20,* 147–157.

Schuh, M. C., Tashie, C., Lamb, P., Bang, M., & Jorgensen, C. M. (1998). Community-based learning for all students. In C. M. Jorgensen (Ed.), *Restructuring high schools for all students: Taking inclusion to the next level* (pp. 209–231). Baltimore: Brookes.

Tashie, C., Jorgensen, C., Shapiro-Barnard, S., Martin, J., & Schuh, M. (1996, September). High school inclusion strategies and barriers. *TASH Newsletter, 22*(9), 19–22.

Team your students for inclusive research outside of school. (1996, August). *Inclusive Education Programs: Advice on Educating Students With Disabilities in Regular Settings, 3,* 1, 10.

Udvari-Solner, A. (1997). Adapting curriculum and instruction in inclusive classrooms. In L. A. Power-deFur & F. P. Orelove (Eds.), *Inclusive education: Practical implementation in the least restrictive environment* (pp. 75–90). Gaithersburg, MD: Aspen.

Wehman, P., Hess, C., & Kregel, J. (1996). Applications for youth with severe disabilities. In P. Wehman (Ed.), *Life beyond the classroom: Transition strategies for young people with disabilities* (2nd ed., pp. 277–301). Baltimore: Brookes.

Ysseldyke, J., & Olsen, K. (1999). Putting alternate assessments into practice: What to measure and possible sources of data. *Exceptional Children, 65,* 175–185.

Conducting Preference Assessments and Reinforcer Testing for Individuals With Profound Multiple Disabilities: Issues and Procedures

Kent R. Logan

Department of Special Education
Kennesaw State University

David L. Gast

Division of Special Education
University of Georgia

The purpose of this article is to review the current research on preference assessment and reinforcer testing for individuals with profound multiple disabilities (PMD). It briefly reviews the literature that describes a subpopulation of individuals with PMD distinct from the general population of individuals labeled as having profound disabilities. The article describes the types of preference assessment procedures that have been used with individuals with PMD. Results from 13 published studies, which assessed preferences and tested reinforcers with individuals with PMD, suggest that preference procedures currently used with individuals at the higher levels of profound disabilities and individuals with severe disabilities are not always successful in identifying preferred stimuli that function as consistent reinforcers for individuals with PMD. Based on this review and other studies over a 3-year period, this article provides a rationale for conducting preference assessments to assist in curriculum development and describes a process for conducting preference assessments and targeting social, affective, and motor behaviors to increase with individuals with PMD.

Researchers consistently have described a subpopulation of individuals with profound disabilities who fall at the extreme lower end of the population of individuals with profound intellectual disabilities. This subpopulation was described by Miller (1976) and Haywood, Meyers, and Switzky (1982) as individuals with "absolute" profound mental retardation, who lacked adaptive behaviors and who existed in a medically fragile state.

Requests for reprints should be sent to Kent R. Logan, 443 Sterling Street NE, Atlanta, GA 30307. E-mail: krlogan1@juno.com

This same subpopulation also was described by Landesman-Dwyer and Sackett (1978) as "nonambulatory, profoundly retarded individuals" (p. 56), who showed high variability in their responses on developmental scales with overall performance below 6 months and low levels of movement characterized by reflexive patterns. Reid, Phillips, and Green (1991) used the term *individuals with profound multiple disabilities* (PMD) to describe this subpopulation. In addition to the previous descriptions, they noted that these individuals, as opposed to individuals who functioned at the higher end of the continuum of individuals with profound disabilities, have a long history of limited progress in learning new skills using traditional systematic instruction procedures, and they will remain totally dependent on caregivers for all aspects of daily living. This definition included individuals who had developmental ages less than 6–8 months; were nonambulatory; had multiple physical, sensory, health, and alertness impairments; and did not use symbolic communication. Following Reid et al., we use the term *individuals with PMD* to describe this subpopulation, and we restricted our review to published articles on preference assessment and reinforcer testing with individuals with PMD.

We reviewed 13 published studies that assessed preferences and tested reinforcers for individuals with PMD. These studies were identified through a hand search of three key journals from the years 1985–1998 that publish studies related to students with PMD: *Journal of Applied Behavior Analysis, The Journal of the Association for Persons With Severe Handicaps,* and *Education and Training in Mental Retardation and Developmental Disabilities.* Additional studies were found through reference lists in those studies and through an ERIC search with the following keyword descriptors: profound disabilities, profound mental retardation, PMD, profound intellectual disabilities, preference assessment, and reinforcement testing.

Three procedures for identifying preferences have been described in the literature for individuals with profound disabilities, in general: successive choice (Pace, Ivancic, Edwards, Iwata, & Page, 1985), forced (paired stimulus) choice (Fisher et al., 1992), and multiple stimulus choice (DeLeon & Iwata, 1996). A summary of this general literature is provided by Hughes, Pitkin, and Lorden (1998). Consistent choice-making behavior is a prerequisite for using either a forced or multiple stimulus choice procedure (Hughes et al., 1998). Most individuals with PMD do not consistently demonstrate choice-making behavior, and they have multiple physical and sensory impairments that make it hard for them to see or interact with multiple stimuli. Therefore, it is not recommended that teachers use forced or multiple stimulus choice procedures with individuals with PMD to assess preferences unless those individuals have adequate motor and visual skills to sample multiple stimuli and have consistent choice-making behavior. All studies that evaluated preferences and reinforcers for individuals with PMD used a successive choice procedure for preference assessment.

Reinforcer testing of the preferred stimulus was conducted by making access to the preferred stimulus contingent on the individual's making specific motor responses. These responses varied from lifting the head to picking up items and placing them on or in a specific container. Preference assessment and reinforcer testing for individuals at the higher end of profound disabilities and for students with severe disabilities have been positive (Hughes et al., 1998). However, the results for individuals with PMD have not been as positive (Ivancic & Bailey, 1996; Logan et al., in press). General results for individuals with PMD across the 13 reviewed studies included the following: (a) Preferred stimuli were found for between 50% and 100% of all individuals; (b) stimuli systematically assessed as preferred functioned more consistently as reinforcers than stimuli thought to be preferred by caregivers; (c) nonpreferred stimuli did not function as reinforcers; (d) some preferred stimuli functioned as reinforcers; (e) some preferred stimuli did not function as reinforcers; (f) some stimuli identified as neutral became preferred over time; (g) reinforcing effects of the preferred stimuli were often variable and not always very strong; (h) individual's hand and arm behaviors for gaining access to stimuli often remained dependent on some continued level of instructor physical prompts; and (i) individual preferences often changed over several weeks and sometimes within a day or session, and individuals demonstrated both habituation and novelty effects (Favell, Realon, & Sutton, 1996; Gast et al., 2000; Green, Gardner, & Reid, 1997; Green & Reid, 1996; Green, Reid, Canipe, & Gardner, 1991; Green et al., 1988; Ivancic & Bailey, 1996; Ivancic, Barrett, Simonow, & Kimberly, 1997; Kennedy & Haring, 1993; Leatherby, Gast, Wolery, & Collins, 1992; Logan et al., 2001; Pace et al., 1985; Realon, Favell, & Lowerre, 1990).

Although it may be difficult to find consistent preferences and reinforcers for individuals with PMD, preference assessment is still critical, because one consistent finding from the reviewed studies was that nonpreferred stimuli do not function as reinforcers. To identify these preferred stimuli, these same researchers have made the following recommendations for conducting preference assessments for individuals with PMD: (a) Teachers and caregivers should conduct a systematic preference assessment rather than rely on subjective opinion about what the individual prefers; (b) some type of preference assessment should be repeated frequently to ascertain if preferences have changed for any individual; (c) preferences should be tested on an ongoing basis to ascertain if they are reinforcers; (d) preferred stimuli should be embedded in ongoing, functional, instructional activities; and (e) preferred stimuli should be used to systematically teach choice-making behaviors.

CONDUCTING PREFERENCE ASSESSMENTS FOR USE IN BUILDING ACTIVE CURRICULA

Hughes et al. (1998) recommended that preference assessments be conducted not as ends in themselves, but for use in curriculum and choice-making instruction for individuals who function at the higher end of profound disabilities and individuals with severe disabilities. We would extend that recommendation to individuals with PMD. Our own work (Logan et al., 1998) suggests that individuals with PMD engaged in higher levels of behavior when the preferred items were incorporated into activities that included typical peers rather than activities with peers with disabilities. Other researchers (Belfliore, Browder, & Mace, 1993) showed that simply involving individuals with PMD in activities increased their alertness and responsiveness, even if systematic preference assessments were not used to develop the activities or the materials used in them. This suggests that the first priority in curriculum development should be an assessment of activities that can be conducted either with typical peers or in stimulating environments. Procedures for conducting these assessments can be found in Logan, Alberto, Kana, and Waylor-Bowen (1994).

We believe that the primary function of a preference assessment for individuals with PMD is to identify preferred stimuli that can be incorporated into the identified activities. For example, a preference assessment might indicate that a student likes vanilla and sour foods and dislikes chocolate and salty foods. Therefore, in conducting a cooking activity, teachers and caregivers should cook or serve items that have vanilla or sour flavors. A second major function of the preference assessment is to identify the sensory system most preferred by the individual and schedule more activities from that sensory system (i.e., a student may like vestibular stimulation more than auditory stimulation). Therefore, it would be important to schedule more motor activities during the day than musical or story-listening activities. For example, with a student who prefers items from the visual system, one might use pompons and colored glue in one art activity, then use neon markers and colored paper in the next, and glitter and colored chalk in the next. The third major function of the preference assessment is to identify as many preferred and neutral items to incorporate into activities so as to capitalize on individuals' increased responding to novel stimuli (preferred and neutral) and to reduce the possibility of habituation (Logan et al., 2001). A fourth function of the preference assessment is to identify items the student finds aversive so as to avoid using them in activities. A fifth function of the preference assessment is to identify neutral and preferred items that can be used to teach contingency responding, one-to-one correspondence, and choice making. For example, a student may like country music but not classical music. Both could be presented in a successive choice fashion prior to a musical activity. Based on the student's longer duration of smiling during country music, the teacher would select that music for use in the activity. A final function of the preference assessment is to identify voluntary affective and motor behaviors that can be increased or maintained during instructional activities. For example, a student may open his or her mouth when he or she is ready for more food but may gaze in the direction of the tape recorder when she wants more music. Therefore, in teaching the communicative function of "more," the teacher would reinforce opening the mouth to indicate more food and eye gaze to indicate more music.

Preference assessments for individuals with PMD should follow procedures described by Pace et al. (1985) or Logan et al. (in press) using a successive choice procedure. In a successive choice procedure, one item at a time is presented in a sequential fashion, and the student's reaction to it is recorded. Individuals typically *approach* the item by smiling at it, reaching for it, looking at it, laughing, touching or playing with it, flaring nostrils and breathing deep, smacking lips, or swallowing it. They *avoid* the item by pushing it away, spitting it out, closing their mouth or eyes, or fussing. They *do not respond* to the item by neither approaching nor avoiding it. An individual's approach to an item can be recorded as either "yes" or "no" (Pace et al., 1985) or by recording the duration of the individual's response to, or interaction with, the item (Logan et al., in press). Because we are looking for items to embed in multiple activities, and to find the individual's favorite sensory system, we want to sample items from all sensory systems in the preference assessment.

Developing a List of Stimuli to Assess

In developing a comprehensive, multisensory list, it is important to consult previous records and to talk with parents, teachers, occupational and physical therapists, speech and language pathologists, itinerant vision and hearing teachers, and peers who interact with individuals with PMD. One should inquire about the types of items (stimuli) and movements they think the student likes and write them down by sensory system. (See Table 1 for a sample list of stimuli by sensory system.) It is important to have between five and eight items that sample the full range of sensory variation within each given system, even if no one mentioned them. Because individuals with PMD are completely dependent on others to bring materials and experiences to them, they simply may not have been exposed to something. For example, no one may have played classical music for an individual, yet she might like it; or, the individual may be too big to hold in your lap and bounce, but he may enjoy being bounced on a miniature trampoline. Perhaps no one ever offered the student a tart flavor or a warm towel. Like us, individuals with PMD might like something they have never tried before.

Conducting the General Preference Assessment

Research consistently has shown that teachers and caregivers are not always accurate in what they think individuals prefer (Green et al., 1988). Therefore, it is important to conduct a general preference assessment to ascertain whether the student actually prefers the items generated for the list. The individual can be assessed either individually or in a group. Almost all of the individuals in our studies showed a preference for social interactions. In fact, for some, the social interaction presented along with another preferred item actually increased or maintained the approach behavior (Logan et al., in press). Because social interactions are an integral part of almost all other interactions, we recommend including these natural social interactions as part of the presentation of the preferred items during the general preference assessment as well as the presession, minipreference assessment described next.

Place the items from each sensory system in a box or make them easily available in the classroom along with a recording sheet with the items listed on it (see Figure 1 for a sample protocol). Make sure the student is positioned appropriately. An assessment session should be between 20 and 45 min, depending on the responsiveness of the student. The total assessment process typically can be completed in three sessions.

Many individuals with PMD take a long time to respond to a given stimulus. This delay can often be 10–15 sec, and presenting the stimulus for only 3–5 sec as originally recommended by Pace et al. (1985) may not give these individuals enough time to approach or avoid the item. Therefore, we recommend the following procedure in conducting the general preference assessment: Present each stimulus sequentially, for 15–30 sec of interaction (for a complete description, see Logan et al., 2001). Fifteen seconds of interaction is recommended for individuals who respond within 5–10 sec, and 30 sec of interaction is recommended for individuals who do not respond for 10–15 sec. This presentation interval should be held constant for all presentations. We also recommend that the person conducting the assessment wait 10–15 sec between the presentation of different items. The duration of the behavior can be timed with a stopwatch or by counting to oneself for as long as the student responds. It may help to have a second person (paraprofessional, typical peer, parent volunteer) watch the student to time the length of the approach behavior and the different approach behaviors the student uses. The assessment session can be videotaped, and

TABLE 1
Stimulus Items by Primary Sensory System

Visual	Auditory	Vestibular	Tactile	Olfactory	Gustatory	Multisensory
Yellow pompon	Fire engine	Vibrators	Brush	Perfume samples	Mashed potatoes with salt	Bouncing
Yellow, furry creature	Lullaby tapes	Swing	Teddy bear	Scented markers	Gatorade	Tickling
Mirror	Boys II Men cassette	Sit up–rock back	Feather boa	Vanilla extract	Apple juice	Socialization
Mechanical dog	Bells	Roll on floor	Fur mouse	Anise extract	Sour cream	Talking
Spinning insect	Kazoos	Invert	Rainbow clown wig	Shaving cream	Chocolate pudding	Praising
Light keychain	Keyalert alarm	Dancing	Dish scrubbies	Coffee	Vanilla pudding	Singing
Moonlight	Noisemaker	Shaking	Mitten with pompon	Menthol		Whispering
Bubbles	Electronic guitar		Lotion			Laughing
Balloon on string			Water			
Mylar wrapping paper			Nail dryer			
Three Little Pigs book			Cold pack			
Mickey Mouse			Heat to Go pack			
wrapped in			Fan			
Christmas lights			Warm Towel			

Student:_____ School:_____
Observers:_____ Dates:_____

Sensory System	Scoring: By each item—write duration, in seconds, of responding, "0" if no response, or "A" if student avoids item.	Behaviors used to indicate approach and avoidance
1. Olfactory	Vanilla	
(Smell)	Coconut	
	Anise	
	Cinnamon	
	Menthol	
	System Duration =	System Total =
2. Tactile	Feather Boa	Behaviors used to indicate approach and avoidance
(Touch)	Hand Lotion	
	Hair Brush	
	Paint Brush (stroking)	
	Paint Brush (dabbing)	
	Bubbles Toward Face	
	Warm Towel	
	Deep Pressure	
	Vibration	
	System Summary =	System Total =
3. Gustatory	Lemon (bitter)	Behaviors used to indicate approach and avoidance
(Taste)	Salty Mashed Potatoes	
	Chocolate Milk	
	Cookies	

FIGURE 1   General Preference Assessment. Adapted from a protocal by Ileana Seoane McCaigue, OTR/L, CDRS and used by permission.

	System Summary =	System Total =
4. Auditory	Taboo Buzzer	**Behaviors used to indicate approach and avoidance**
(Hearing)	Rap Music	
	Story/Oz on Tape	
	Hard Rock	
	Soft Classical	
	Soft Rock	
	Latin	
	System Summary =	System Total =
5. Visual	Flashlight	**Behaviors used to indicate approach and avoidance**
(Seeing)	Camera Flash	
	Mirror	
	4 Pictures in Folder	
	System Summary =	System Total =
6. Vestibular	Gentle Rocking	**Behaviors used to indicate approach and avoidance**
(Movement)	Protective Response–Back	
	Protective Response–Forward	
	Prone Rocking Over a Ball	
	Quadruped on Table or Floor	
	System Summary =	System Duration =
7. Multisensory	Bouncing	**Behaviors used to indicate approach and avoidance**
	Tickling	
	Social–Verbal Talk	
	Social–Verbal Praise	
	Social–Singing	
	Social–Whispering	
	System Summary =	System Total =

FIGURE 1 (Cont.)

the durations of the behaviors can be timed while watching the tape. To use the protocol (see Figure 1), record (a) how many seconds the individual approached the item, (b) "zero" if the student did not respond to the item, or (c) "A" if the individual avoided the item. In addition, record what behavior the student used to indicate approach or avoidance to the item. Present each item once during each assessment session, and conduct two sessions. To score the protocol, add the duration of responding from each of the two sessions for each item, and record the total duration under "system summary." Divide the system summary by the total number of items assessed. This is the "system total." The sensory system with the largest system total is the most preferred sensory system and the one with the shortest system total is the least preferred. Make a list of the items the student approached, starting with those with the highest system totals. These are the student's preferred items. Make a separate list of the items for which there was no response. These are the student's neutral items. Do not use the items that were avoided.

We believe that the primary reason for conducting the preference assessment with individuals with PMD is to identify preferred and neutral items to be used in activity-based instruction. As discussed earlier, the first step in developing activity-based curriculum is to develop and schedule a variety of activities. The second step is to develop a materials list based on preferred and neutral items from the general preference assessment for each activity. The third step is to schedule a majority of activities that represent the student's favorite sensory system and that includes a large number of preferred items. These activities should include typical peers to the maximum extent possible (Logan et al., 1998) and be conducted in a variety of settings, including the community (Logan et al., 1994).

A second reason to conduct the preference assessment is to identify the approach behaviors individuals with PMD used to indicate a preference. We believe that these behaviors should form the core of the instructional program for individuals with PMD, and they should be targeted for instruction within the context of the selected activities. These are often the only motor behaviors over which many individuals with PMD have voluntary control. Increasing these approach behaviors is important because these are typically the behaviors associated with increased alertness, affect (happiness), social interaction, early nonsymbolic communication, and choice making. These behaviors are also the foundation for higher level skills (Sailor, Gee, Goetz, & Graham, 1988). In addition, these behaviors are important to increase and maintain because they consistently are described as indicating an improved quality of life (Felce & Perry, 1995).

Reinforcer Testing

Previous research with individuals with PMD suggests that preferred items may not function as reinforcers. Therefore, it is necessary to complete reinforcer testing of the preferred items (for a complete description of reinforcer testing, see Pace et al., 1985). Given that the preferences of individuals with PMD often change over time, we recommend that this reinforcer testing be conducted on an ongoing basis within the context of instructional activities rather than as a separate assessment. Because preferences change over time, it is essential to continually monitor the reinforcing value of the preferred items. This ongoing assessment of reinforcer value through data collection should be an integral part of instruction.

Conducting Presession, Minipreference Assessments to Determine the Most Preferred Stimulus

Research has shown that the preferences of individuals with PMD can change not only over a few weeks, but also within the course of 1 day or even during a 30-min activity (Kennedy & Haring, 1993). These individuals also demonstrate habituation and novelty effects (Logan et al., 2001). Because it is important to use preferred items (student responding is always higher if we use them), teachers and caregivers should reassess the student frequently to make sure they are always using preferred items. We recommend that presession, minipreference assessments should be completed on an ongoing basis prior to various activities to identify items most preferred at that time (see Gast et al., 2000). This presession assessment also teaches initial choice-making behavior.

To complete a presession assessment, create a box for each student with four to six preferred and neutral items for each scheduled activity based on the comprehensive preference assessment. During the presession assessment, choose two preferred and two neutral items from the box that are related to the upcoming activity. It is important to include both preferred and neutral items in the presession assessment to prevent satiation and to be able to provide novel items that might be preferred. In addition, by presenting neutral items along with preferred items, we are teaching the student how to make personal choices. Previous research suggests that allowing the student to choose between only preferred items may not be any different than having someone else make the choice (Smith, Iwata, & Shores, 1995). With consistent contingent pairing of the approach behavior indicating preference for an item and the use of that item in the immediately following activity, the student may learn that his or her differential response during the presession assessment to preferred and neutral items leads to increased access to that most preferred stimulus.

During the presession assessment, present two preferred and two neutral items in a random order to the individual. Present each of the four items to the student for 15 sec. Maintain verbal interaction that encourages the student to look at, touch, reach for, smile at, or laugh at the item. Record how long the student approaches each item. Wait 5–10 sec before presenting the next item. After all four items have been presented, choose the item with the longest duration of the approach behavior as the most preferred item, and use it to try to increase that approach behavior or another targeted behavior in the instructional session immediately following. By conducting these presession assessments frequently, teachers can find the currently preferred stimuli for use in activities and increase the chances of optimal student responding (for a complete description of presession assessment, see Gast et al., 2000).

CONCLUSIONS

Individuals with PMD present the ultimate challenge to teachers in teaching basic developmental skills, finding items or movements that they like, developing stimulating curriculum activities based on those items and movements, and teaching new skills or increasing or maintaining current skills. Given the difficulty in teaching these individuals, it is critical that teachers use instructional procedures that have been documented to be effective with individuals with PMD. This article reviewed the research on preference assessment and reinforcer testing with individuals with PMD. This review suggests that although preferred stimuli do not always function as reinforcers and that preferred items change over time for individuals with PMD, it is still important to identify preferred stimuli because neutral stimuli do not function as reinforcers. The general preference assessment helps teachers and caregivers develop an extended list of preferred and neutral stimuli across all sensory systems that can be embedded in activity-based instruction. The ongoing (presession) assessment helps teachers and caregivers find stimuli that are preferred at a given moment in time and that can be embedded in specific instructional activities immediately following the presession assessment. Presession assessment also teaches choice making, which is an important skill for individuals with PMD to learn. By employing these procedures, teachers can build more effective instructional environments for individuals with PMD.

ACKNOWLEDGMENTS

This research was supported by U.S. Department of Education Grant H023C40115. However, the opinions expressed do not necessarily reflect the policy of the U.S. Department of Education, and no official endorsement by the U.S. Department of Education should be inferred.

REFERENCES

Belfliore, P. J., Browder, D. M., & Mace, F. C. (1993). Effects of community and center-based settings on the alertness of persons with profound mental retardation. *Journal of Applied Behavior Analysis, 26*, 401–402.

DeLeon, I., & Iwata, B. (1996). Evaluation of a multiple-stimulus presentation format for assessing reinforcer preferences. *Journal of Applied Behavior Analysis, 29*, 519–533.

Favell, J., Realon, R., & Sutton, K. (1996). Measuring and increasing the happiness of people with profound mental retardation and physical handicaps. *Behavioral Interventions, 11*(1), 47–58.

Felce, D., & Perry, J. (1995). Quality of life: Its definition and measurement. *Research in Developmental Disabilities, 16*, 51–74.

Fisher, W., Piazza, C., Bowman, L. G., Hagopian, L. P., Owens, J. C., & Slevin, I. (1992). A comparison of two approaches for identifying reinforcers for persons with severe and profound disabilities. *Journal of Applied Behavior Analysis, 25*, 491–498.

Gast, D. L., Jacobs, H. A., Logan, K. R., Murray, A. S., Holloway, A. H., & Long, L. (2000). Pre-session assessment of preferences for students with profound multiple disabilities. *Education and Treatment in Mental Retardation and Developmental Disabilities, 35*, 393–405.

Green, C. W., Gardner, S. M., & Reid, D. H. (1997). Increasing indices of happiness among people with profound multiple disabilities: A program replication and component analysis. *Journal of Applied Behavior Analysis, 30*, 217–228.

Green, C. W., & Reid, D. H. (1996). Defining, validating, and increasing indices of happiness among people with profound multiple disabilities. *Journal of Applied Behavior Analysis, 29*, 67–78.

Green, C. W., Reid, D. H., Canipe, V. S., & Gardner, S. M. (1991). A comprehensive evaluation of reinforcer identification processes for persons with profound multiple handicaps. *Journal of Applied Behavior Analysis, 24*, 537–552.

Green, C. W., Reid, D. H., White, L. K., Halford, R. C., Brittain, D. P., & Gardner, S. M. (1988). Identifying reinforcers for persons with profound handicaps: Staff opinion versus systematic assessment of preferences. *Journal of Applied Behavior Analysis, 21*, 31–43.

Haywood, H. C., Meyers, C. E., & Switzky, H. N. (1982). Mental retardation. *Annual Review of Psychology, 33,* 309–341.

Hughes, C., Pitkin, S. E., & Lorden, S. W. (1998). Assessing preferences and choices of persons with severe and profound mental retardation. *Education and Training in Mental Retardation and Developmental Disabilities, 33,* 299–316.

Ivancic, M. T., & Bailey, J. S. (1996). Current limits to reinforcer identification for some persons with profound multiple disabilities. *Research in Developmental Disabilities, 17,* 77–92.

Ivancic, M. T., Barrett, G. T., Simonow, A., & Kimberly, A. (1997). A replication to increase happiness indices among some people with profound multiple disabilities. *Research in Developmental Disabilities, 18,* 79–89.

Kennedy, C. H., & Haring, T. G. (1993). Teaching choice making during social interactions to students with profound multiple disabilities. *Journal of Applied Behavior Analysis, 26,* 63–76.

Landesman-Dwyer, S., & Sackett, G. P. (1978). Behavior changes in nonambulatory, profoundly mentally retarded individuals. In C. E. Meyers (Ed.), *Quality of life in severely and profoundly retarded people: Research foundations for improvement* (pp. 55–144). Washington, DC: American Association on Mental Deficiency.

Leatherby, J. G., Gast, D. L., Wolery, M., & Collins, B. C. (1992). Assessment of reinforcer preference in multi-handicapped students. *Journal of Developmental and Physical Disabilities, 4,* 15–36.

Logan, K. R., Alberto, P. A., Kana, T. A., & Waylor-Bowen, T. (1994). Curriculum development and instructional design for students with profound disabilities. In L. Sternberg (Ed.), *Individuals with profound disabilities: Assistive and instructional strategies* (pp. 417–454). Austin, TX: PRO-ED.

Logan, K. R., Jacobs, H. A., Gast, D. L., Murray, A. S., Daino, K., & Skala, C. (1998). The impact of typical peers on the perceived happiness of students with profound multiple disabilities. *The Journal of The Association for Persons With Severe Handicaps, 23,* 309–318.

Logan, K. R., Jacobs, H. A., Gast, D. L., Smith, P. D., Daniel, J., & Rawls, J. (2001). Preferences and reinforcers for students with profound multiple disabilities: Can we identify them? *Journal of Developmental and Physical Disabilities, 13,* 97–122.

Miller, C. R. (1976). Subtypes of the PMR: Implications for placement and progress. In C. C. Cleland, J. D. Swartz, & L. W. Talkington (Eds.), *The profoundly mentally retarded* (pp. 57–61). Austin, TX: Western Reserve Conference and Hogg Foundation.

Pace, G. M., Ivancic, M. T., Edwards, G. L., Iwata, B. A., & Page, T. J. (1985). Assessment of stimulus preference and reinforcer value with profoundly retarded individuals. *Journal of Applied Behavior Analysis, 18,* 249–255.

Realon, R. E., Favell, J. E., & Lowerre, A. (1990). The effects of making choices on engagement levels with persons who are profoundly multiply handicapped. *Education and Training in Mental Retardation and Developmental Disabilities, 25,* 299–305.

Reid, D. H., Phillips, J. F., & Green, C. W. (1991). Teaching persons with profound multiple handicaps: A review of the effects of behavioral research. *Journal of Applied Behavior Analysis, 24,* 319–336.

Sailor, W., Gee, K., Goetz, L., & Graham, N. (1988). Progress in educating students with the most severe disabilities: Is there any? *The Journal of The Association for Persons With Severe Handicaps, 13,* 87–99.

Smith, R. G., Iwata, B. A., & Shores, B. A. (1995). Effects of subject versus experimenter selected reinforcers on the behavior of individuals with profound developmental disabilities. *Journal of Applied Behavior Analysis, 28,* 61–71.

Customizing Instruction to Maximize Functional Outcomes for Students With Profound Multiple Disabilities

Pamela D. Smith

Civitan International Research Center
University of Alabama at Birmingham

David L. Gast

Division of Special Education
University of Georgia

Kent R. Logan

Department of Special Education
Kennesaw State University

Heidi A. Jacobs

Decatur City Schools

This article describes a process for customizing instruction for students with profound multiple disabilities that has been used to design instructional programs and maximize the attainment of functional outcomes for students. The process focuses on collaborative teamwork and problem solving to design and implement instructional programs by ensuring that the 5 components of the process are included. Team members determine (a) prepositioning handling procedures; (b) overall body positioning for instruction; (c) hand, arm, and head positioning; (d) instructional adaptations and materials; and (e) handling procedures to combine with systematic instructional strategies.

Providing a quality educational program for students with profound multiple disabilities that is functional, integrated, and outcome oriented can be extremely difficult and complicated for educators and related services personnel. Students with profound multiple disabilities have impairments that are "serious and dramatic, and they may include signifi-

Requests for reprints should be sent to Pamela D. Smith, University of Alabama at Birmingham, Civitan International Research Center, SC 208, 1530 3rd Avenue South, Birmingham, AL 35294–0017. E-mail: Psmith@civmail.circ.uab.edu

cant or total sensory impairment in addition to very severe cognitive impairments, severe physical disabilities, chronic health impairments, and sometimes terminal illness" (Ferguson, Willis, & Meyer, 1996, p. 100). Historically, these students have been referred to as children with multiple disabilities and are an important subgroup of students referred to in special education literature as having "severe disabilities" (Orelove & Sobsey, 1996; Reid, Phillips, & Green, 1991). For many of these students, identification of a single voluntary response (e.g., eye gaze; small movement of hand, arm, or head) is extremely difficult. Therefore, students with profound multiple disabilities require extensive special education and related services (e.g., physical therapy) provided by personnel who must have expertise in their own discipline, as well as an understanding of the role, responsibilities, and techniques of related disciplines. The responsibility of each discipline representative is to adapt his or her own instruction and service provision to best meet the needs of the student.

Many programs continue to provide instruction and related services for these students in a passive manner that emphasizes therapy goals rather than integrated therapy services that facilitate the attainment of educational goals, and to use multidisciplinary or interdisciplinary models that lack sufficient collaborative teamwork and coordination of services. Such programs are inefficient at best and often result in a lack of attainment of functional outcomes for these students to affect their daily lives and the lives of their families. In addition, many special educators and related services personnel lack sufficient training, expertise, and experience in working with students with profound multiple disabilities.

The transdisciplinary model has gained wide acceptance by programs for students with profound multiple disabilities and across a variety of disciplines. "The model is characterized by a sharing, or transferring, of information and skills across traditional disciplinary boundaries" (Orelove & Sobsey, 1996, p. 11) and incorporates an indirect therapy approach whereby therapists function as consultants to the teacher and other team members in addition to providing direct services as needed. In addition, an indirect therapy approach includes role release, which involves the sharing of information and teaching of skills across traditional disciplinary boundaries and releasing of some roles of one discipline to other team members. One example is physical therapists teaching other team members correct positioning for students (Lyon & Lyon, 1980; United Cerebral Palsy Association, 1976). As depicted in Figure 1, we view the classroom teacher as the educational synthesizer and primary service provider performing the roles of coordinator of the team and facilitator of service delivery (Bricker, 1976), with other team members acting as consultants in customizing instruction for students with profound multiple disabilities.

This article describes a process for customizing instruction for students with profound multiple disabilities that has been used to design instructional programs and maximize the attainment of functional outcomes for students. The process embodies four primary principles: teacher serving as team facilitator and coordinator of service delivery, collaborative teamwork and transdisciplinary service delivery (Orelove & Sobsey, 1996; Rainforth & York-Barr, 1997; Smith, 1990), functional assessment, and applied creative problem solving. The components of this process are presented in Figure 2 and provide a framework for team members to efficiently and effectively pool their expertise and focus

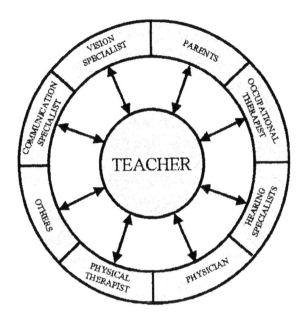

FIGURE 1   Organization of transdisciplinary team approach with the classroom teacher as the primary service provider and team coordinator.

their efforts on customizing instruction to achieve functional outcomes for students and their families. Classroom teachers may use these components as a guide for questions to ask consulting therapists and specialists or as areas in need of their expertise for assessment and problem solving. For teachers, completing this process for all students across all target objectives requires coordination and dedication of some time, typically several weeks with one-on-one ongoing problem solving on a regular basis throughout the school year with other team members.

GETTING STARTED

First, review students' records for at least the past 3 years, especially Individualized Education Programs goals and objectives, assessment reports and recommendations, progress reports, and outside evaluations (e.g., private consultants, hospital, university program). While reviewing these records, take notes using the student assessment summary format shown in the Appendix. Typically, teachers compile this information, then share and consult with other team members based on their areas of expertise, or teachers may ask team members to complete the section that applies to their area of expertise and then compile the information to share with all team members. Either way, completing and sharing this information is an effective and efficient way for team members to familiarize themselves with each student as a "whole person," including strengths and needs across skill areas (i.e., motor, communication, etc.).

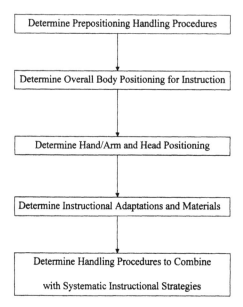

FIGURE 2   Components of process for customizing instruction for students with profound multiple disabilities.

Next, team members select a functional outcome or *target behavior* for the student on which to focus. Priority is based on the primary concern of the student's family and preferences of the student, such as the use of a switch to activate battery-operated toys or a cassette player for music, stories, or family members' voices on tape; self-feeding with a spoon; or eye-gaze for choice making. The student's target behaviors become the focal point for all team members as they apply their efforts and expertise in a collaborative team approach across the instructional planning components described in the following sections. Each of these components takes time, trial and error, observation, and team collaboration.

DETERMINE PREPOSITIONING HANDLING PROCEDURES

The first component is to determine if prepositioning handling procedures are required prior to static positioning and instructional sessions. The term *handling* is used to describe hands-on techniques used to normalize muscle tone, facilitate upright positions and normal posture, and facilitate normal movements. For example, many students require therapeutic handling or dynamic positioning to normalize muscle tone and promote proper positioning (e.g., hips, trunk, shoulders) to place the student in a quality static position or in positioning equipment (Rainforth & York-Barr, 1996). Students with high muscle tone (hypertonia, spasticity, rigidity) may require handling procedures such as trunk rotation, slow rocking or rolling, or warmth via a blanket prior to positioning to reduce muscle tone enough to obtain flexion (bending) of the hips and lower extremities (knees) to attain proper positioning with normal posture. The efforts of physical and occupational therapists must focus on determining the most effective handling procedures for students and training other team members to implement these across instructional activities as needed. Teachers may want to obtain videotaped segments of the therapist performing the prepositioning handling procedures with individual students to review as needed after the initial training has been conducted. Resources to consult on prepositioning handling procedures include Finnie (1975), Jaeger (1987), Rainforth and York-Barr (1996), and Wright and Bigge (1991).

DETERMINE OVERALL BODY POSITIONING FOR INSTRUCTION

The second component in customizing instruction for students with profound multiple disabilities is to determine optimal positioning needed for instruction. Positioning provides postural support to normalize muscle tone, maintains alignment and posture, improves the quality and quantity of purposeful or goal-directed movements of distal body parts (i.e., hands, arms, and head), and increases participation in meaningful activities (Rainforth & York-Barr, 1996; Ward, 1984; Wright & Bigge, 1991). Positioning options include stomach lying (prone), back lying (supine), side lying, supported sitting (e.g., wheelchair, feeder seat, floor sitter), kneeling, and standing (e.g., prone stander, supine stander, standing frame). Observe and assess the student's performance in each possible position, noting the quality and quantity of motor output (Smith, 1989). The position chosen must provide the student enough postural support to (a) normalize tone, (b) minimize interfering abnormal movements (e.g., associated reactions, extension), (c) facilitate goal-directed movements (e.g., hand, arm, or head movements to activate a switch), and (d) allow the student to concentrate his or her efforts on participation in the activity instead of on maintaining body posture. This position also must (a) match the target behavior, (b) be similar to the position that peers without disabilities use for the activity, and (c) not interfere with the student's functional vision and hearing abilities (Utley, 1994). In addition, the student's positioning preferences and behavior state (Guess et al., 1988) are considered. For example, students who are primarily drowsy or sleepy may benefit from an upright seated position to increase alertness versus a more relaxed, reclined, or lying position. The main goal here is to choose the position for instruction that creates the optimal conditions to promote the student's best performance while being appropriate for the instructional activity and setting. Both physical and occupational therapists are trained in positioning, and educators and other team members who have not had sufficient training in this area must be taught basic positioning techniques to implement across activities throughout the school day for all students who require them. In addition, we suggest that teachers obtain photographs of the positioning for individual students to promote consistency and to train other team members. Excellent resources to consult on positioning include Finnie (1975), Ward, and Wright and Bigge.

DETERMINE HAND, ARM, AND HEAD POSITIONING

The third component is to determine the hand, arm, and head positioning needed to promote the movements required to perform the target behavior. In general, if hand and arm movements are used and the student lacks sufficient head control to focus on the task, the student's head must be supported by providing head and neck supports or physical assistance so that the student's efforts are devoted to participation in the activity and not on maintaining his or her head erect. When hand, arm, or head movements are used in the target activity, slightly round the student's shoulders forward, position the arms toward midline, and provide a supporting surface (e.g., lap tray) of optimal height (i.e., upper and lower arm creates a 90° angle). Some students may require small wedges or rolled towels behind the upper arms, or elbow blocks on their wheelchair or lap tray to assist in midline positioning of the arms and hands. Students whose arms exhibit increased extension may benefit from an inclined surface that provides additional flexion of the arms to normalize muscle tone and promote hand, arm, or head movements. Examples of inclined support surfaces include wooden slant boards, inclined wedges, and inclines from cardboard boxes. Sometimes a vertical pommel or dowel may be needed to stabilize a student's nondominant hand to assist him or her in maintaining a stable upright position, thus improving the function of the dominant hand. To promote controlled head movements and minimize extraneous arm and trunk movements, the trunk and arms may need to be stabilized by positioning the student's arms under the lap tray (Trefler, 1982) or stabilizing both arms using an inclined support surface, as described earlier, with or without the use of hand-held pommels or dowels, as appropriate (Goossens' & Crain, 1992). Teachers must work collaboratively with occupational therapists who have expertise in positioning to promote arm, hand, and head movements, as well as skill in developing hand splints, which can be extremely beneficial in improving hand function for many students.

DETERMINE INSTRUCTIONAL ADAPTATIONS
AND MATERIALS

The fourth component involves determining instructional adaptations and materials. Adaptations can range from very inexpensive ones, such as using velcro to secure a switch on a lap tray, to expensive, commercially available switch-mounting systems and electronic communication devices. However, most adaptations are inexpensive or can be constructed easily with a little imagination and ingenuity. It is not within the scope of this article to adequately describe how to select and adapt instructional materials for all students with profound multiple disabilities. However, several key considerations need to be addressed when selecting instructional materials and conducting switch assessments for students with profound multiple disabilities.

Selecting Instructional Materials

Selection of instructional materials is based on two guiding factors: students' preferred sensory input modalities (i.e., visual, auditory, vestibular, tactile, olfactory, or gustatory) and preferences for specific items or stimuli. Basic information on student preferences can be gathered by asking parents and significant others in addition to classroom observation and information gathered from other team members. In addition, teachers can conduct a more formal or systematic assessment of preferences using multiple stimuli across all sensory modalities (Logan et al., 2001; Mason & Egel, 1995; Pace, Ivancic, Edwards, Iwata, & Page, 1985). The results can provide an array of preferred materials and activities for instructional purposes (e.g., reinforcers) and critical information regarding students' preferred sensory modality as a starting point for selecting instructional materials. However, preference assessment is an ongoing activity, because student preferences change over time. In addition, teachers must work closely with vision and hearing specialists to determine specific adaptations needed for students with sensory impairments to maximize their functional vision and hearing abilities (Langley, 1996; Utley, 1994).

An additional team consideration is that instructional materials be positioned appropriately based on students' visual and physical abilities and limitations. Many students need instructional materials presented at a 30–40° angle for ease of viewing and physical manipulation, as opposed to positioning materials lying flat and horizontal. In addition, instructional materials may need to be positioned to the student's left or right side for students who are able to see or reach materials primarily on one side of the body (Utley, 1994).

Conducting Switch Assessments

If adaptive switches are to be used, switch assessments must be conducted to determine a viable switch setup that the student can perform reliably using a voluntary movement with as normal movement patterns as possible and minimal fatigue. Switch assessments consist of three main components: movement pattern selection, switch selection, and positioning the switch (Goossens' & Crain, 1992). Informal observation techniques are used by the teacher in collaboration with physical and occupational therapists to conduct switch assessments by observing students' (a) typical motor performance during routine activities with familiar persons to determine a reliable movement pattern and control site (e.g., exact contact point on the student's hand, head, or foot), (b) activation of an array of switches that can be operated using the selected movement pattern and control site, and (c) efficiency in activating the switch in a variety of locations to determine the mounting format. Ideally, hand activation of switches is preferred over other control sites (e.g., head, foot), because hand activation appears less "different," and activation of switches using head movements can trigger involuntary and detrimental changes in muscle tone and posture for some students. Switches then are mounted appropriately for students using commercially available switch mounts or low-cost mounting materials such as velcro, nonslip materials (e.g., dycem, rug pad), ethafoam, and plastic plumbing pipe. Various low-cost mounting formats with construction specifications are described in detail by Goossens' and Crain as well as others (Wright & Bigge, 1991; York-Barr, Rainforth, & Locke, 1996).

DETERMINE HANDLING PROCEDURES TO COMBINE WITH SYSTEMATIC INSTRUCTION STRATEGIES

The final component is to determine handling procedures to be used during instruction in combination with systematic physical prompting strategies (e.g., graduated guidance, most-to-least prompts, backward chaining). These handling procedures are hands-on techniques that "facilitate normal movements including (a) automatic movements that maintain balance, (b) locomotion of independent mobility, (c) arm and hand movements for task performance, and (d) oral movements for eating and speech" (Rainforth & York-Barr, 1996, p. 83), while maintaining normal muscle tone and postures or positioning. Handling techniques must be individually designed to meet the unique movement needs of a particular student and are based on the student's type and degree of physical or motor disability and how it interferes with performing the target behavior. For example, many students with cerebral palsy move in total patterns of movement (e.g., they are unable to isolate hand movements from total arm movements) or lack the ability to move their arms due to extreme tightness in the shoulder caused by high muscle tone. These students may benefit from handling procedures that facilitate movement patterns by involving the entire upper limb using key points of control (shoulder, elbow, wrist, fingers) to (a) normalize muscle tone and attain; (b) maintain alignment of the upper limb; and (c) physically guide or prompt the student to perform the target, goal-directed arm movement. Handling techniques fade as students' movement patterns improve. Examples of other handling procedures can be found in Finnie (1975) and Rainforth and York-Barr.

When therapeutic handling procedures are used in combination with systematic instruction in meaningful, reinforcing activities with students with multiple and motor disabilities, their performance improves significantly (Campbell, McInerney, & Cooper, 1984; Giangreco, 1986). Physical and occupational therapists can design and train teachers to implement handling procedures that can be incorporated into physical prompting strategies to improve student performance. We suggest that teachers and therapists videotape these procedures so that teachers and others can ensure that they are performing the handling procedure correctly and consistently.

FINALIZING THE INSTRUCTIONAL SETUP AND PUTTING IT ALL TOGETHER

After team members have addressed the previous components for customizing instruction, an individualized instructional program is developed for each student that includes the student's individual setup, instructional strategy, and data collection procedures. The instructional setup includes a description of the target behavior, positioning, prepositioning preparation and handling, positioning for hand and arm function or head control, instructional adaptations and materials, and handling required during instruction.

CASE STUDY

Allie is 4 years, 6 months old, and functions cognitively at 1–4 months and below a 6-month level across all other developmental areas (refer to the Appendix). She has severe spastic cerebral palsy as well as bilateral hearing loss, seizures, asthma, and chronic respiratory congestion. She demonstrated no controlled voluntary movements of the head or extremities (i.e., arms, legs). Allie's functional outcome or target behavior was to activate a switch with her hand using a slight arm movement (approximately 1–2 in.) to access her preferred toys (e.g., lighted snowman, bunny). Allie's teacher worked collaboratively with Allie's team members and designed her instructional setup as follows.

Prepositioning Handling Procedures

Remove Allie's ankle–knee–foot orthoses. Position her prone over the green therapy ball; provide 5 min of slow, rhythmic rolling and rocking (relaxation, tone reduction).

Overall Body Positioning for Instruction

Position Allie in sidelyer, on her right side with her back and pelvis against back of sidelyer, and her upper body rotated slightly forward (the slight trunk rotation reduces muscle tone). Secure the trunk belt and position a small pillow under her head, using dycem to maintain the pillow in place. Position her bottom (right) leg straight and her top (left) leg flexed at the hip and knee and resting on a wedge. Wait approximately 5 min for her body to adjust to the position.

Hand and Arm Positioning

Teacher does "arm warm-up" before applying hand splint or positioning arm, and repeats this during the session, as needed, to "break up" tone. Arm warm-up consists of any combination of the following: (a) Apply deep pressure on left shoulder; (b) flex and extend left arm; (c) rotate flexed shoulder at elbow up and down; and (d) "shake" arm while flexing moving shoulder backward, then pull or extend arm forward at shoulder. After the arm warm-up, apply hand splint to left hand and position left arm over small roll to prevent excessive shoulder flexion due to high muscle tone.

Instructional Adaptations and Materials

Attach the AbleNet Big Red switch to the inclined, metal bookend (secured with velcro). Attach the bookend switch mount to the small box for correct height (secured with velcro). Place the teacher-made snowman edged with small colored Christmas lights approximately 24 in. away from Allie's face. Connect the switch and lights to the AbleNet control unit, and plug the control unit's power cord into an electrical outlet.

Handling Procedures to Combine With Systematic Instructional Procedures

Place one hand on Allie's shoulder to promote shoulder flexion, and place the other hand above Allie's wrist to provide stabilization. Allie's hand should be 2 in. above the center of the switch at the beginning of each instructional trial. Use the arm warm-up techniques as needed.

When Allie's teacher implemented this customized instructional setup that addressed her multiple needs, Allie exhibited voluntary arm movements of her left arm to activate the switch to access her favorite toys.

SUMMARY

Customizing instruction for students with profound multiple disabilities is a tremendous challenge for educational teams, and it is crucial in providing an appropriate educational program for these students. We encourage teachers and educational teams to use the components described in our process as a framework for team problem solving and collaborative teamwork to design and implement educational programs that truly result in the attainment of functional outcomes for these students and their families.

ACKNOWLEDGMENTS

This study was supported by Grant H023C40115 to the University of Georgia, Department of Special Education by the U.S. Department of Education and Rehabilitative Services Field-Initiated Research Program. However, the opinions expressed do not necessarily reflect the Policy of the U.S. Department of Education, and no official endorsement by the U.S. Department of Education should be inferred.

REFERENCES

Bricker, D. (1976). Educational synthesizer. In M. A. Thomas (Ed.), *Hey, don't forget about me!* (pp. 84–97). Reston, VA: Council for Exceptional Children.

Campbell, P., McInerney, W., & Cooper, M. (1984). Therapeutic programming for students with severe handicaps. *American Journal of Occupational Therapy, 38,* 594–602.

Ferguson, D. L., Willis, C., & Meyer, G. (1996). Widening the stream: Ways to think about including "exceptions" in schools. In D. H. Lehr & F. Brown (Eds.), *People with disabilities who challenge the system* (pp. 99–112). Baltimore: Brookes.

Finnie, N. (1975). *Handling the young cerebral palsied child at home* (2nd ed.). New York: Dutton.

Giangreco, M. (1986). Effects of integrated therapy: A pilot study. *Journal of the Association for Persons With Severe Handicaps, 11,* 205–208.

Goossens', C., & Crain, S. S. (1992). *Utilizing switch interfaces with children who are severely physically challenged.* Austin, TX: PRO-ED.

Guess, D., Ault, M. M., Roberts, S., Struth, J., Siegel-Causey, E., Thompson, B., Bronicki, G. J., & Guy, B. (1988). Implications of biobehavioral states for the education and treatment of students with the most profoundly handicapping conditions. *The Journal of the Association for Persons With Severe Handicaps, 13,* 163–174.

Jaeger, L. (1987). *Home program instruction sheets for infants and young children.* Tucson, AZ: Communication Skill Builders.

Langley, M. B. (1996). Screening and assessment of sensory functions. In M. McLean, D. B. Bailey, & M. Wolery (Eds.), *Assessing infants and preschoolers with special needs* (2nd ed., pp. 123–164). Columbus, OH: Prentice Hall.

Logan, K. R., Jacobs, H. A., Gast, D. L., Smith, P. D., Daniels, J., & Rawls, J. (2001). Assessing preferences and reinforcers for students with profound multiple disabilities: Can we identify them? *Journal of Developmental and Physical Disabilities, 13,* 97–122.

Lyon, S., & Lyon, G. (1980). Team functioning and staff development. A role release approach to providing integrated educational services for severely handicapped students. *Journal of the Association for the Severely Handicapped, 5,* 250–263.

Mason, S. A., & Egel, A. L. (1995). What does Amy like? Using a mini-reinforcer assessment to increase student participation in instructional activities. *Teaching Exceptional Children, 28*(1), 42–44.

Orelove, F. P., & Sobsey, D. (1996). *Educating children with multiple disabilities: A transdisciplinary approach* (3rd ed.). Baltimore: Brookes.

Pace, G. M., Ivancic, M. T., Edwards, G. L., Iwata, B. A., & Page, T. J. (1985). Assessment of stimulus preference and reinforcer value with profoundly retarded individuals. *Journal of Applied Behavior Analysis, 18,* 249–255.

Rainforth, B., & York-Barr, J. (1996). Handling and positioning. In F. P. Orelove & D. Sobsey (Eds.), *Educating children with multiple disabilities: A transdisciplinary approach* (3rd ed., pp. 79–118). Baltimore: Brookes.

Rainforth, B., & York-Barr, J. (1997). *Collaborative teams for students with severe disabilities: Integrating therapy and educational services* (2nd ed.). Baltimore: Brookes.

Reid, D. H., Phillips, J. F., & Green, C. W. (1991). Teaching persons with profound multiple handicaps: A review of the effects of behavioral research. *Journal of Applied Behavioral Analysis, 24,* 319–336.

Smith, P. D. (1989). Assessing motor skills. In D. B. Bailey & M. Wolery (Eds.), *Assessing infants and pre-schoolers with handicaps* (pp. 301–338). Columbus, OH: Merrill.

Smith, P. D. (1990). *Integrating related services into programs for students with severe and multiple handicaps.* Lexington: Interdisciplinary Human Development Institute, University of Kentucky.

Trefler, E. (1982). Arm restraints during functional activities. *American Journal of Occupational Therapy, 36,* 599–600.

United Cerebral Palsy Association. (1976). *Staff development handbook: A resource for the transdisciplinary process.* New York: Author.

Utley, B. L. (1994). Providing support for sensory, postural, and movement needs. In L. Sternberg (Ed.), *Individuals with profound disabilities: Instructional and assistive strategies* (3rd ed., pp. 123–191). Austin, TX: PRO-ED.

Ward, D. E. (1984). *Positioning the handicapped child for function* (2nd ed.). Chicago: Phoenix Press.

Wright, C., & Bigge, J. (1991). Avenues to physical participation. In J. L. Bigge (Ed.), *Teaching individuals with physical and multiple disabilities* (3rd ed., pp. 132–174). New York: Macmillan.

York-Barr, J., Rainforth, B., & Locke, P. (1996). Developing instructional adaptations. In F. P. Orelove & D. Sobsey, *Educating children with multiple disabilities: A transdisciplinary approach* (3rd ed., pp. 119–159). Baltimore: Brookes.

APPENDIX
Assessment Summary for Allie

NAME: Allie   TEACHER: S. Nelson   SCHOOL: Hopkins Elementary
DOB: 3/21/90   AGE: 4–6   ATTENDANCE: Excellent
DEVELOPMENTAL LEVELS: Gross Motor: 2m   Fine Motor: 0–1m   Communication: 2–6m
   Cognition: 1–4m   Social: 5–6m Self-Help: < 6m
PRIMARY DISABILITY: Profound multiple disabilities
SECONDARY DISABILITIES & HEALTH STATUS:
Motor Disability: severe spastic cerebral palsy, quadraplegic
   Interfering Reflexes—associated reactions primarily to the left
   Head Control—requires full support, tonic head turning
   Hand/Arm Use—extreme tightness/hypertonicity in shoulders, arms, hands; no voluntary use of upper limbs
   Optimal Positioning—sidelying; wheelchair or positioning chair, slightly reclined
Visual Impairments: unknown, none specified
Hearing Impairments: moderate bilateral (50–70 dB)
Special Health Care Needs: gastrostomy feeding (Kangaroo pump), feeding time 1.5 hr; asthma, chronic congestion
Nutrition/Feeding: tonic bite reflex, tongue thrust; takes some foods & liquids orally
Seizures: grand mal, controlled by phenobarbital
Medications (side effects): phenobarbital (potential side effects include confusion, unusual excitement)
SPECIAL EDUCATION & RELATED SERVICES: physical therapy (30 hr/year); occupational therapy
   (20 hr/year); speech–language therapy (1 hr/week)
STIMULATORY OR AGGRESSIVE BEHAVIORS: none
STUDENT PREFERENCES: familiar people and peers, socialization more than objects; lighted objects and
   toys, having picture taken, peek-a-boo
CURRENT NEEDS:
Communication: switch use with supported hand/arm activation, plus vocalizations during play
Feeding: decrease oral sensitivity via oral stimulation both outside and inside mouth; increase tolerance of
   various food textures
Environmental/Sensory: decrease tonal increases and resistance to tactile stimuli
Movement/Positioning: increase head in midline to attend to activity, maintain ROM in all four extremities,
   tolerate positioning for 30 min across three different positions
STRENGTHS:
Focuses & fixates—people, light/visuals
Tracks—people, body movements, objects (vertical, horizontal to midline, does not cross midline)

Meeting the Communication Needs of Students With Severe and Multiple Disabilities in General Education Classrooms

June E. Downing
Department of Special Education
California State University, Northridge

The importance of communication skills for students with the most significant disabilities is highlighted. Specific attention is paid to the need to recognize and understand the unconventional means of communication that a particular student may be using. Those around the student build on this present skill performance by being responsive to all communicative efforts by the student, making use of different naturally occurring opportunities, providing different means for communication, and recognizing the reinforcing nature of social interactions. Allowing students with significant disabilities to be more than requesters of items by giving them other ways to share information about themselves is addressed. Some ideas for augmenting the student's communicative efforts are provided, as well as the critical importance of team collaboration to support the student's efforts.

Communication is an essential skill for all human beings, allowing us to learn from others, have control over our environment, share feelings, and develop friendships. Yet, for some individuals, due to the severity of their disabilities, expressing even basic needs can require a significant effort. Although everyone does communicate, individuals with severe and multiple disabilities may not have full access to or full control of the multiple means by which most individuals express themselves (e.g., speech, facial expressions, body language, print; Downing, 1999). When individuals demonstrate minimal communication skills that are difficult to understand, the tendency may be to assume that they have nothing to say (Biklen, 1993; Crossley, 1992). Such an assumption is dangerous in that it dehumanizes individuals, placing them in dependent positions. Following a less dangerous assumption, all individuals should be perceived as having something to say despite the difficulty in doing so. It is the responsibility of educators and all team members

Requests for reprints should be sent to June E. Downing, California State University, 18111 Nordhoff Street, Northridge, CA 91330–8265. E-mail: june.downing@csun.edu to help these individuals communicate by providing appropriate motivation, keeping expectations high, and letting individuals with disabilities know that what they have to say (however it is said) is valued.

Communication, simply stated, is the exchange of a message between a sender and a receiver, such that the message is understood (Butterfield & Arthur, 1995). Besides this obvious social aspect, communication requires a form (i.e., a way to send the message), content (i.e., something to talk about), and a reason or purpose (Gruenewald, Schroeder, & Yoder, 1982). Beyond these basic components, no special skill is needed. Furthermore, there is neither one correct way to communicate, nor only one reason to communicate, nor one topic to discuss. Individuals communicate about many different things, with different people, for different purposes, and in many different forms.

Speech is not a requirement for communication and, in fact, much of any message between people may be communicated via nonsymbolic or nonabstract means (Evans, Hearn, Uhlemann, & Ivey, 1984). This is good news for the student with severe and multiple disabilities who has not acquired a symbolic mode of expression, whether speech, sign, pictures, or print. Such students can and still do engage in communication. They simply may need greater assistance to be understood, because the form of communication that they may use may be highly esoteric and difficult to discern. For example, one student may rock his head from side to side when he has a headache, whereas another student does the same behavior when he is enjoying some music. Some students with the most significant disabilities may use breath control and some muscle tension to convey yes and no. Unfortunately, adults may find it difficult to recognize communicative efforts by students with very significant disabilities (Houghton, Bronicki, & Guess, 1987; Walden, Blackford, & Carpenter, 1997). Careful observation and assessment of how students are communicating without additional support is needed so that all team members know how to recognize the communicative potential and intent, and then build on some skills.

INTERPRETING COMMUNICATIVE BEHAVIOR FOR GREATER PARTNER RESPONSIVITY

When communication is somewhat unconventional and at times difficult to interpret, an adaptation may be needed to ensure consistency of responding across team members. Mirenda (1999) advised the development and use of a gesture dictionary. This dictionary offers an interpretation of a student's communicative behavior with suggestions for appropriate responding. The dictionary can be in a book or chart format and alphabetized by the behavior (e.g., R for rocking) or by the intent of the behavior (e.g., H for headache), depending on team members' preference and ease of access. Information is divided among three columns: the behavior of the student, the interpretation of this behavior, and how the communication partner is to respond. An example of some entries in a gesture dictionary for a student is presented in Table 1. This dictionary is a dynamic device that grows with the student. It should be kept in the student's portfolio and move from grade to grade with the student.

TABLE 1
Sample From a Communication Dictionary

What Ben Does	What It Means	How to Respond
Pounds the wheels on his chair	"I want you to put the brakes on."	Set his wheelchair brakes and let him push himself.
Puts his fist on his chest	"I want."	Ask him what he wants by giving him some choices.
Shakes head side to side	"I have a headache."	Give him some aspirin.

ENHANCING THE SOCIAL ENVIRONMENT

Obviously, responsive communication partners are needed so that students' communicative efforts are not ignored or overlooked. Responsive partners need to increase their proximity to the student, obtain eye contact (or tactile contact), look expectantly at the student, give the student sufficient time to initiate or respond, avoid being overly directive, and accept the student's current mode of communication (Downing, 1999). The typical general education classroom (preschool through high school) tends to offer a highly social environment with a variety of potential communication partners as well as diverse and interesting topics for discussion. Experts in communication intervention stress the value of teaching communication skills in general education classrooms where students with severe disabilities have the support of their peers (Calculator & Jorgensen, 1994; Janney & Snell, 1996; Mirenda, 1993). Students with no disabilities not only model appropriate communication, but also can respond quickly to the communicative efforts of their classmate with severe disabilities, assist in interpreting what this student is trying to say, and use effective strategies that maintain conversational exchanges (e.g., asking questions). Classrooms that use different instructional groupings such as cooperative learning, small-group instruction, buddy systems, and centers tend to encourage and support greater student interactions than classrooms that stress independent seatwork and large-group instruction led by the teacher (Johnson & Johnson, 1991; Putnam, 1998). Therefore, when there is an option, students with significant disabilities should be placed in classrooms that will meet their communication needs for frequent communication opportunities and the presence of responsive partners.

TAKING ADVANTAGE OF NATURALLY OCCURRING OPPORTUNITIES WITHIN THE CLASSROOM

Instead of doing repetitive discrete trial training on specific communication skills (e.g., requesting an item) in a distraction-free, specialized environment, the many opportunities that naturally exist in a general education classroom should be used. Team members need to take advantage of the teachable moments that occur during each day to address communication skills (Downing, 1999). For example, regardless of the student's age, several opportunities exist daily to teach social greetings and farewells. For this function of communication, students with severe and multiple disabilities require a quick way to interact, either aided or unaided.

Multiple opportunities exist throughout each day for students to request certain actions, items, or people. Students can request help to engage in an activity, specific items or materials to use within activities, places to sit or be positioned, specific activities, types of snacks and lunch items, and certain students with whom to work or play. Individuals who support these students need to remember to offer these types of choices instead of making such decisions for students. Although it may be faster for the adult to decide what materials a student will use, what activity a student will do, where a student will be positioned, and so on, the opportunities to teach critical communication skills is lost. Furthermore, the control obtained by the student when allowed to make a choice and have a request met is typically reinforcing for the student, thus encouraging the student to acquire this skill more rapidly. In addition, students typically draw attention to themselves throughout the day. Students without disabilities typically do this by raising their hand or approaching others. Students with severe physical disabilities who cannot engage in these behaviors will require an alternative method, such as the use of a switch operated voice output communication aid that says the message, "Come see what I've got!" or "I'd really like to talk to someone." Several daily opportunities are available for students to make use of this type of message.

Regardless of ability level, students typically have very clear ways of rejecting or protesting. Students may cry, push things off their desks, drop items, throw themselves on the floor, or run off. Although their means of saying no may not be conventional, students with severe and multiple disabilities should be given opportunities throughout each day to express their desire to not engage in an activity. Several opportunities exist in general education classrooms at all age levels, and support providers simply must make use of these opportunities and allow the student his or her right to express this purpose of communication. Sigafoos and Roberts-Pennell (1999) described a strategy of specifically presenting "wrong" items to students with developmental disabilities to give them the opportunity to learn to reject. Of course, if the student expresses "no" in such a way that it is distracting for the rest of the class or is harmful to others, oneself, or materials, then the team will want to provide an alternative and more conventional means of allowing this student to express this rejection. For example, one student wears a fanny pack with a symbol for "No, I don't want to" attached to it. When he hits this symbol, demands are removed temporarily and other options provided. In this way, he can say no without having to resort to somewhat violent and undesirable behavior.

In typical classrooms, students without disabilities are constantly making comments, sharing information, asking questions, and engaging in interactions for a purely social intent (e.g., teasing, joking). Opportunities for these types of interactions occur during breaks in more structured activities, during recess and lunch or nutrition breaks, while transitioning from one class to another, right before and after school, and during cooperative learning and paired learning situations. Although students with severe and multiple disabilities may be part of the "action" and close to their peers without disabilities, they may be perceived as not being able to perform this function of communication. As a result, they may not be given the means to truly share in these types of interactions other than what facial expressions, eye contact, and simple gestures can convey. For instance,

Elizabeth, a seventh grader, would like to express her interest in makeup and clothes, but because she is perceived by others only to be able to request items, she has not been given any means of expressing this interest. She can only request them; she cannot talk about them or ask anyone else about them.

Recognizing the opportunities that naturally exist for communicative exchanges is the first step in any intervention. Determining how to help the student to make the most use of these opportunities will be a team effort. Because identifying natural opportunities to teach communication skills to students with severe and multiple disabilities may not always be obvious to some (Sigafoos, Kerr, Roberts, & Conzens, 1994), analyzing the natural environment specifically for this purpose is a critical skill for team members. Careful observation of how and when same-age peers engage in communication can serve as a basis for intervention. Assessing each student's ability to meet communication demands and expectations within typical social environments will help to determine where the students will need to be taught skills and whether augmenting the student's present communication behavior is needed. Being creative with regard to augmentative communication devices is a critical skill for those interested in helping students with severe and multiple disabilities gain the most from their interactions with others.

COMMUNICATION IS MORE THAN SAYING "I WANT"

Communication intervention for students with the most complex disabilities typically begins with teaching them how to make basic requests. In fact, a communication device for a particular student may contain only those symbols that allow that student to make requests. This, in turn, limits those around the student to asking what that student wants. The interaction goes no further than satisfying basic needs. Teaching students with severe and multiple disabilities to request using aided and unaided means may be targeted often due to a greater ease in instruction, and obvious and immediate gratification for the student (McDonnell, 1996; Sanchez-Fort, Brady, & Davis, 1995). Recognizing ways for children to make requests throughout the day may be easier than determining how they will meet other communication needs, such as sharing information about themselves, teasing, or asking questions.

Although communication intervention often has addressed the student's need to make basic requests, an equal need involves interactions for social closeness (Light, 1997). Students need to be able to form relationships with others rather than just make requests. They need to be allowed to let others know who they are, what they like, and how they feel about things. They also need to be able to joke and tease and interact for the pure joy of interacting. To address this issue, Hunt, Alwell, and Goetz (1991) and Hunt, Farron-Davis, Wrenn, Hirose-Hatae, and Goetz (1997) demonstrated how the use of conversation books as augmentative communication devices helped students with severe and multiple disabilities form relationships with their peers with no disabilities. As part of the educational team, students without disabilities were trained in methods of keeping the conversation going by asking questions and making comments that their friend with severe disabilities could respond to using the conversation book. Although the purpose of communication to request desired items is certainly critical, it is insufficient in meeting all of the needs of students with disabilities. Rather, a critical goal of education for students with severe disabilities is to help them develop friendships with their classmates who do not have disabilities (Haring & Breen, 1992; Strully & Strully, 1996).

AUGMENTING THE COMMUNICATION EFFORTS OF STUDENTS WITH SIGNIFICANT DISABILITIES

The student who does not use speech to convey messages will require adaptations to allow participation in the social interactions of the classroom. Augmentative communication devices provide a means for students without speech to share information with their peers as well as satisfy basic needs. Such devices can involve considerable complex technology or can be quite simple and easy to use. Their design and development will depend on a number of factors, including the student's cognitive, physical, and visual abilities, as well as the student's needs and preferences. Analyzing the communicative environment of the student's typical day provides practical information regarding what a student may need to say, for what purposes, when, and to whom. When the student's unaided communication skills (e.g., facial expressions, gestures, vocalizations) cannot adequately address the demands of the environment, then some type of communication device will be needed. This becomes particularly evident when the student is trying to convey something other than requests.

Designing Augmentative Communication Devices

Devices need to (a) reflect the age of the student, (b) reflect the way that others of the same age express themselves, (c) be easy to use, (d) be available when needed, and (e) meet the needs of the social environment. As critical members of the team, the student's peers can assist with the development of the device so that it sounds more like the student and not an adult. Given the multimodal nature of communication in general, the student probably will rely on many different ways to communicate. These should be encouraged, and a strict adherence to just one modality or device should be avoided. It is important to remember that even highly skilled augmentative communication device users often rely on and prefer nonsymbolic methods of communication, such as gestures and facial expressions (Murphy, Markova, Moodie, Scott, & Bon, 1995). The goal of communication intervention is to assist individuals in understanding others and expressing their thoughts and ideas, not to master any specific technological aid (Beukelman, 1991). What is critical, however, is that students who do make use of a particular device or devices have those aids made available at all times and not just when it is convenient for adult supporters.

Types of Augmentative Communication Devices

Depending on the needs and abilities of the student, and the demands of the environment, the communication device could be in the form of a small book, large notebook, box, CD holder, small board, videocassette holder, wristband, bracelet, small photograph album, or a variety of different types of voice output communication aids. The size will depend on whether it needs to be portable and how many symbols it needs to display. For example, a 4th-grade student who is deaf–blind and has a hemiplegia form of cerebral palsy, but is quite active, may prefer to wear a wristband with a few symbols on it when he goes outside with his class for recess, physical education, and lunch. He does not like carrying devices, and so this works well for him. Another student, Crissy, is a 10th grader who uses a wheelchair and has very limited vision. She uses a notebook and a choice board that hold objects and parts of objects to make requests and to tell her classmates about herself. She also uses a BIGmack (a voice output device) to call others to her, because she cannot get to them easily.

Deciding how messages will be portrayed is a critical step in developing an augmentative communication device. Symbols used on devices could be in the form of photographs, black-and-white line drawings, colored pictures from magazines or advertisements, a commercial product such as Boardmaker® (Mayer Johnson, Solana Beach, CA), or a student's own drawings if the student has sufficient vision to make use of these symbols. Symbols also could be in the form of objects or parts of objects, depending on what best represents the referent from the student's perspective. If the student does not have usable vision, then those deciding what symbols will be used should assume a tactile perspective and not a visual one. For example, representing the use of a computer through the presentation of an actual computer disk may make more sense to the student who uses the disk than a miniaturized computer that only *looks* like a computer and does not *feel* like one. Whenever possible, it is always beneficial to obtain same-age peer input on symbol selection as well as the student's own preferences.

Regardless of what symbol is used to represent the intended message, words or sentences should be added so that the message is understood more easily by others (Downing, 1999). Without the written message, considerable confusion is possible. For instance, a student who points to the picture of a book could be requesting a story, stating that he or she likes a particular story, asking if the other person likes to read, asking where a book is, or telling the person that story time is next. Adding words greatly clarifies for the receiver, who then will be better able to respond appropriately and maintain the interaction. How words are added should reflect how typical same-age peers would sound if making similar statements. For example, a high school student seems to enjoy sports. He uses a notebook full of pictures taken from sport sites on the Internet, baseball cards, pictures from magazines, and photographs that his family has taken to convey his interest in particular teams, ask classmates if they know who won a particular game, ask them if they want to hear a joke about sports, and relate information regarding recent activities he has done. This notebook has the most recent *Sports Illustrated*, with a note attached asking if anyone wants to look at it. His friends who share his interest in sports help to keep this communication device updated and of interest to others.

THE NEED FOR A TEAM APPROACH

Because communication opportunities exist throughout the day and can occur at any time and place and involve many people, the need for a collaborative team effort is apparent. Teaching effective communication skills is a challenging endeavor and requires the input and effort of everyone involved. Certainly, family members and friends need to be actively involved in the identification of communication needs and the demands of different environments. They also play a valuable role in determining the best way for a student to express certain things. Based on his or her experiences, training, knowledge, and unique perspectives, each individual team member can contribute in a meaningful way to addressing the communicative needs of the student. The benefits of team members working in a collaborative fashion has been well documented (Giangreco, Edelman, Luiselli, & MacFarland, 1996; Rainforth & York-Barr, 1997; Utley, 1993).

When everyone is equally involved in addressing the communication needs of the student, there is greater commitment to this critical area of intervention and much greater consistency across team members. In addition, different team members observe the student in different social environments throughout the day. They witness different interactions that require specific vocabularies and different modes of expression. This compilation of information from different sources provides a rich basis for effective communication intervention across settings and situations.

Classmates as Team Members

Perhaps the most critical members of the team are the student's classmates. These students essentially provide the rich social environment and multiple opportunities to communicate. Students with and without disabilities share daily experiences, which is crucial to supporting social interactions (Durand, Mapstone, & Youngblade, 1999). Students engaged in common school activities have common referents to discuss. They can bemoan an unpopular lunch, ask questions about an assignment, complain about a substitute teacher, express interest and excitement over a science experiment, and become immersed in a play or book being read. Although some classmates without disabilities have natural skills at interacting with their classmates who do not use speech, others need more assistance in this regard (Bedrosian, 1997; Davis, Reichle, Johnston, & Southard, 1998; Hunt et al., 1997). Students without disabilities may need to be specifically instructed about how their classmate communicates and for what purposes, how they should respond to maintain the interaction, and what they can do to help support their classmate's communicative efforts. Given the number of students without disabilities who possibly could come in contact with the student having severe and multiple disabilities, it is critical that we make effective use of this very valuable and available resource.

SUMMARY

Placing students with severe and multiple disabilities in general education classrooms is not the goal, but the premise, a foundation. As part of this learning environment, they have the right to an appropriate education. It is not enough just to be there; students must be learning. This right requires that those members of the educational team take advantage of the rich and supportive learning environment and specifically address critical learning needs. Effective communication skills (both receptive and expressive) are critical for learning in all other areas.

When students have extremely challenging difficulties understanding others and making their needs known, those around them (their communication partners) will need to assume primary responsibility for supporting the interaction (Bedrosian, 1997). Communication partners need to be not only especially responsive to any communicative attempt (regardless of the form of the communication), but also creative in determining ways for the student to convey more effectively the intended message. Although there is no prescribed intervention for all students with complex needs, there are many creative ideas. We must recognize that what students are trying to tell us is worth the effort needed to improve our present intervention strategies, so that their voices can be heard more clearly.

REFERENCES

Bedrosian, J. (1997). Language acquisition in young AAC system users: Issues and directions for future research. *Augmentative and Alternative Communication, 13,* 179–185.

Beukelman, D. (1991). Magic and cost of communication competence. *Augmentative and Alternative Communication, 7,* 7–20.

Biklen, D. (1993). *Communication unbound.* New York: Teachers College Press.

Butterfield, N., & Arthur, M. (1995). Shifting the focus: Emerging priorities in communication programming for students with a severe intellectual disability. *Education and Training in Mental Retardation and Developmental Disabilities, 30,* 41–50.

Calculator, S. N., & Jorgensen, C. M. (1994). *Including students with severe disabilities in schools: Fostering communication, interaction, and participation.* San Diego, CA: Singular.

Crossley, R. (1992). Getting the words out: Case studies in facilitated communication training. *Topics in Language Disorders, 12*(4), 46–59.

Davis, C. A., Reichle, J., Johnston, S., & Southard, K. (1998). Teaching children with severe disabilities to utilize nonobligatory conversational opportunities: An application of high-probability requests. *The Journal of the Association for Persons With Severe Handicaps, 23,* 57–68.

Downing, J. E. (1999). *Teaching communication skills to students with severe disabilities.* Baltimore: Brookes.

Durand, V. M., Mapstone, E., & Youngblade, L. (1999). The role of communication partners. In J. E. Downing (Ed.), *Teaching communication skills to students with severe disabilities* (pp. 139–156). Baltimore: Brookes.

Evans, D., Hearn, M., Uhlemann, M., & Ivey, A. (1984). *Essential interviewing: A programmed approach to effective communication* (2nd ed.). Pacific Grove, CA: Brooks/Cole.

Giangreco, M. F., Edelman, S. W., Luiselli, T. E., & MacFarland, S. Z. C. (1996). Support service decision making for students with multiple service needs: Evaluative data. *The Journal of the Association for Persons With Severe Handicaps, 21,* 135–144.

Gruenewald, L., Schroeder, J., & Yoder, D. (1982). Considerations for curriculum development and implementation. In B. Campbell & V. Baldwin (Eds.), *Severely handicapped/hearing impaired students: Strengthening service delivery* (pp. 163–179). Baltimore: Brookes.

Haring, T., & Breen, C. (1992). A peer-mediated social network intervention to enhance the social integration of persons with moderate and severe disabilities. *Journal of Applied Behavior Analysis, 25,* 319–333.

Houghton, J., Bronicki, G. J., & Guess, D. (1987). Opportunities to express preferences and make choices among students with severe disabilities in classroom settings. *The Journal of the Association for Persons With Severe Handicaps, 12,* 18–27.

Hunt, P., Alwell, M., & Goetz, L. (1991). Interacting with peers through conversation turn taking with a communication book adaptation. *Augmentative and Alternative Communication, 7,* 117–126.

Hunt, P., Farron-Davis, F., Wrenn, M., Hirose-Hatae, A., & Goetz, L. (1997). Promoting interactive partnerships in inclusive educational settings. *The Journal of the Association for Persons With Severe Handicaps, 22,* 127–137.

Janney, R. E., & Snell, M. E. (1996). How teachers use peer interactions to include students with moderate and severe disabilities in elementary general education classes. *The Journal of the Association for Persons With Severe Handicaps, 21,* 72–80.

Johnson, D. W., & Johnson, R. T. (1991). *Cooperative learning lesson structures.* Edina, MN: Interaction Book Company.

Light, J. (1997). Communication is the essence of human life: Reflections on communicative competence. *Augmentative and Alternative Communication, 13,* 61–70.

McDonnell, A. P. (1996). The acquisition, transfer, and generalization of requests by young children with severe disabilities. *Education and Training in Mental Retardation and Developmental Disabilities, 31,* 213–234.

Mirenda, P. (1993). AAC: Bonding the uncertain mosaic. *Augmentative and Alternative Communication, 9,* 3–9.

Mirenda, P. (1999). Augmentative and alternative communication techniques. In J. E. Downing (Ed.), *Teaching communication skills to students with severe disabilities* (pp. 119–138). Baltimore: Brookes.

Murphy, J., Markova, I., Moodie, E., Scott, J., & Bon, S. (1995). Augmentative and alternative communication systems used by people with cerebral palsy in Scotland: Demographic survey. *Augmentative and Alternative Communication, 11,* 26–36.

Putnam, J. W.(1998). *Cooperative learning and strategies for inclusion: Celebrating diversity in the classroom* (2nd ed.). Baltimore: Brookes.

Rainforth, B., & York-Barr, J. (1997). *Collaborative teams for students with severe disabilities: Integrating therapy and educational services* (2nd ed.). Baltimore: Brookes.

Sanchez-Fort, M. R., Brady, M. P., & Davis, C. A. (1995). Using high-probability requests to increase low-probability communication behavior in young children with severe disabilities. *Education and Training in Mental Retardation and Developmental Disabilities, 30,* 151–165.

Sigafoos, J., Kerr, M., Roberts, D., & Conzens, D. (1994). Increasing opportunities for requesting in classrooms serving children with developmental disabilities. *Journal of Autism and Developmental Disabilities, 24,* 631–645.

Sigafoos, J., & Roberts-Pennell, D. (1999). Wrong-item format: A promising intervention for teaching socially appropriate forms of rejecting children with developmental disabilities? *Augmentative and Alternative Communication, 15,* 135–140.

Strully, J. L., & Strully, C. (1996). Friendships as an educational goal: What we have learned and where we are headed. In S. Stainback & W. Stainback (Eds.), *Inclusion: A guide for educators* (pp. 141–154). Baltimore: Brookes.

Utley, B. L. (1993). Facilitating and measuring the team process within inclusive educational settings. *Clinics in Communication Disorders, 3*(2), 71–85.

Walden, T. A., Blackford, J. U., & Carpenter, K. L. (1997). Differences in social signals produced by children with developmental disabilities of differing etiologies. *American Journal of Mental Retardation, 102,* 292–305.

Integrating Preference Assessment Within the Transition Process to Create Meaningful School-to-Life Outcomes

Sharon Lohrmann-O'Rourke

Department of Special Education
Marywood University

Ophelia Gomez

College of Education and Human Services
Lehigh University

The Individuals With Disabilities Education Act mandates the provision of transition services to adolescent students with disabilities who are leaving school to enter the adult world. For students with severe disabilities who use limited symbolic or nonsymbolic communication, it may be difficult to accurately interpret desired school-to-life outcomes. The purpose of this article is to discuss the inclusion of systematic preference assessment within transition planning as a way to accurately interpret the preferences of students who use limited symbolic or nonsymbolic communication means. By using person-centered planning as a framework, this article illustrates how to embed preference assessment within transition planning so that the Individualized Education Program team can follow the leads and needs of the focus student. Special considerations are offered as they relate to preference assessment and transition planning.

The Individuals With Disabilities Education Act (IDEA) mandates the provision of transition services to adolescent students with disabilities who are leaving school to enter the adult world. Embedded in IDEA's definition of transition services are three key elements: (a) transition outcomes; (b) planning processes; and (c) student's needs, interests, and preferences. The first key element, transition outcomes, pertains to the individual's lifestyle defined as a person's preferred way of living his or her life. Transition outcomes or goals aim to teach more than a set of skills; rather, they may be perceived as the way of life chosen by the adolescent to embark on after leaving school.

Requests for reprints should be sent to Sharon Lohrmann-O'Rourke, Marywood University, 2300 Adams Avenue, Scranton, PA 18509–1598. E-mail: lohrman@es.marywood.edu

Transition outcomes can be classified broadly into four domains: living, working, playing, and learning. In the living domain, competencies targeted are those required to participate in the community and live independently (e.g., domestic skills and accessing community resources). Included in the working domain are those competencies involved in finding and maintaining a job (e.g., task-specific skills or job tryouts). Although not included as a transition outcome in IDEA, the playing domain involves competencies necessary to participate in recreation or leisure activities. Finally, the learning domain provides for ongoing education and includes specific outcome areas such as adult continued education and postsecondary education. Embedded within are the social dimensions (e.g., developing relationships or day-to-day interactions) natural to each of these domains that enable the student to interact successfully with people such as coworkers, roommates, or activity partners. For the focus student to become a fully functioning member of the community after leaving school, targeting outcomes in all four domains is significant.

Implicit in these transition outcomes are essential quality-of-life issues that come about because of one's chosen lifestyle. Inherent in the quality of transition outcome is the degree to which these goals promote community inclusion of students. For example, community living is more than a roof over one's head; it means being a contributing member of the community, establishing a valued role that gains others' respect, and exercising choice making in daily living (O'Brien, 1987). Being in the community is not the same as being part of the community (Taylor & Bogdan, 1989). The former refers to physical presence, whereas the latter addresses establishing personal and social relationships. In a similar light, Walker (1999) raised other critical issues that adults with disabilities living in the community experience as they move from being physically integrated to a sense of belonging, such as safety, familiarity, and being known and accepted. Although Furney, Hasazi, and De Stefano (1997) found that participants in their study viewed transition planning as a "natural extension" of the inclusion concept, in reality, Grigal, Test, Beattie, and Wood (1997) noted that integration in the workplace and recreation settings was less evident.

Despite empirical examples (Hughes et al., 1997) and the importance of transition goals and their accompanying quality-of-life issues, actual transition plans lack quality, defined goals, and elements of best practice. For example, Grigal et al. (1997) found that transition goals were stated vaguely or too broadly (e.g., "will think about best place to live, will explore jobs") for team members to even make specific plans (deFur, Getzel, & Kregel, 1994; Grigal et al., 1997).

The aforementioned results highlight several needs for transition goals that go beyond mere and minimal compliance with IDEA (Baer, Simmons, & Flexer, 1996; Grigal et al., 1997). First, for adolescent students to develop into well-rounded individuals, transition goals need to be comprehensive and holistic, in that goals should target all four domains (i.e., living, working, playing, and learning). Second, transition goals need to go beyond annual accomplishments and address planning needs across the years (Grigal et al., 1997). Finally, transition goals need to reflect inclusionary practices that go beyond mere physical community presence.

The second key element to transition is the planning process. IDEA's "coordinated set of activities" points to the need for a systematic planning process to facilitate students' transition (Blackorby & Wagner, 1996; Wehmeyer & Lawrence, 1995). One approach well suited to the transition process is person-centered planning, because it allows for identification of the student's needs and preferences, and emphasizes the importance of life quality (Everson, 1996; Miner & Bates, 1997; Mount & Zwernick, 1988). The benefits of person-centered planning have been discussed widely and offer transition teams an approach designed to break down the system barriers often experienced when planning major lifestyle decisions (e.g., waiting lists or limited funding) with individuals with severe disabilities (Mount, 1994). Typically, a person-centered planning approach includes the following steps: (a) development of a personal profile, (b) vision planning, and (c) action planning. In transition planning, the use of this approach has enhanced parents' participation, but factors such as procedural requirements and limited time allotment for meetings may discourage comprehensive discussion of transition issues (Miner & Bates, 1997). To ensure comprehensive outcomes, there is a need to provide open and ongoing discussion opportunities throughout the transition-planning process.

Finally, the third key element in the transition process is the individual's needs, interests, and preferences. In planning for one's lifestyle, assessment of the individual's preferences is particularly crucial, because preference gives value and meaning to the chosen lifestyle. According to IDEA, these aspects of the individual "shall be taken into consideration" when planning for transition. This provision presupposes the need for assessment of the individual. However, assessment, particularly preference assessment, in transition planning often is overlooked or neglected (Lichtenstein, 1993; Lichtenstein & Michaelides, 1993; Sitlington, Neubert, & Leconte, 1997). When included, assessment of preference usually is limited to vocational interests (Morgan, Moore, McSweyn, & Salzberg, 1992).

Although self-determination and preference are inextricably intertwined, both Morgan et al. (1992) and Wehmeyer and Schwartz (1998) found a lack of focus on assessing the individual's self-determination needs. At the very core of being self-determined is the knowledge and awareness of oneself and one's preferences (Field & Hoffman, 1994). To act in self-determined ways is then, in turn, an expression of those preferences.

In summary, there is a need to systematically link all three key elements within transition planning. This is especially true for those students with the most severe disabilities, who will require intensive planning to achieve desirable postschool outcomes. One approach is to weave in preference assessment throughout the planning process, considering lifestyle outcomes in all four domains. Given such a need, the purpose of this discussion is to illustrate how to integrate preference assessment within the transition process using person-centered planning as a framework to promote meaningful school-to-life outcomes for students with severe and profound disabilities. This article extends the literature on preference assessment in several ways, including suggesting the use of a team planning format, embedding systematic preference assessment within person-centered planning approaches to facilitate the transition process, and offering an approach for assessing abstract and complex lifestyle decisions.

OVERVIEW OF SYSTEMATIC PREFERENCE ASSESSMENT

Systematic preference assessment refers to a process that involves selecting options for sampling, providing sampling opportunities, and observing the individual's response to the option. His or her response then is interpreted as a relative indicator of preference or nonpreference. In a review of the literature, Lohrmann-O'Rourke and Browder (1998) identified four core features present across studies on preference assessment: context, sampling options, selection responses, and presentation format. The assessment context refers to the schedule and location in which the assessment occurs. Lohrmann-O'Rourke, Browder, and Brown (2000) recommended presenting sampling options distributed across the day within the natural context whenever possible. The second feature, assessment stimuli, refers to the actual items or events identified for sampling. Selection responses refers to the behaviors observed when in the presence of the sampling options. Typically, responses are defined as discrete behaviors (e.g., points to item) or as a multicomponent definition (e.g., Dyer, 1987). Hughes, Pitken, and Lorden (1998) noted that many studies include collateral responses (e.g., time on task) to further enhance definitions of preference. Finally, the assessment format refers to how the sampling options are presented to the person (e.g., one at a time, in pairs or arrays).

INTEGRATING PREFERENCE ASSESSMENT IN TRANSITION PLANNING

When preferences are assessed and included in formal planning, the goals and objectives designed are more likely to reflect the individual's personal preference (Newton, Horner, & Lund, 1991). Further, implicit in person-centered planning is the belief that the planning process should follow the lead and needs of the focus student (Butterworth et al., 1993; Everson, 1996; Hagner, Helm, & Butterworth, 1996; Mount, 1994; Mount & Zwernick, 1988). Traditionally, person-centered planning team members design a vision for the future based on their knowledge of the focus student and what they think the student wants. Because it may be very difficult to interpret and honor expressions of preference for individuals with limited communicative ability, the risk of misinterpreting expressions of preference or nonpreference greatly increases (Brown, Gothelf, Guess, & Lehr, 1998; Butterfield & Arthur, 1995; Lohrmann-O'Rourke et al., 2000). Because of this, we believe that focus students need systematic opportunities to sample potential lifestyle options so that they can be better prepared to express their own opinions about a vision for the future.

Embedding systematic preference assessment within the transition-planning process allows the focus student to explore the many possibilities that exist for their future. To integrate preference assessment (see Table 1), the team begins the transition process by creating a picture or profile of the focus student based on team members' relationships and knowledge of the student. Using this information, the team creates an initial long-term vision and generates a list of possible lifestyle options for sampling. Then, a systematic preference assessment is conducted, providing the focus student with opportunities to sample available options. The team then finalizes the vision using the information obtained through the preference assessment and plans for action.

Knowing the Focus Student

Consistent with person-centered planning strategies, the first step is to develop a profile that provides a rich description of the focus student (Mount & Zwernick, 1988). Because

TABLE 1A

Transition Planning Using Systematic Preference Assessment

Step 1: Knowing the Person (VINE)	Step 2: Planning the Initial Vision	Step 3: Conducting the Preference Assessment	Step 4: Finalizing the Vision and Plan
Describe the students	Develop a vision using VINE to guide the team.	Define a sampling schedule.	Finalize a vision based on the focus student's preferences.
Values and beliefs	Define the characteristics of each major lifestyle component of the vision.	Create nontraditional sampling experiences.	Develop a plan that addresses the support and skill needs to achieve the desired outcomes.
Interests and preferences	Generate a list of sampling options for each major lifestyle component of the vision.	Obtain commitments from all members.	
Natural and paid supports		Develop time lines for completion.	
Expertise and abilities		Ensure accurate interpretation: Define the communicative responses, including preference, nonpreference, and termination that will be observed. Consider effects of partner or option familiarity.	

TABLE 1B
Strategies to Increase Focus Student Participation Throughout the Planning Process

Step 1: Knowing the Person (VINE)	Step 2: Planning the Initial Vision	Step 3: Conducting the Preference Assessment	Step 4: Finalizing the Vision and Plan
Summarize the information in a format that the focus person can understand.	Prepare the focus student so that he or she can share what is important to him or her during vision planning.	Involve the focus student in developing the sampling schedule.	Summarize the information in a format the focus student can understand.
	Have the student in a position of leadership (e.g., start the meeting, signal topic changes) during the meeting.	Listen to and honor behaviors that may be expressing termination or dissatisfaction.	Prepare the focus student to share his or her preferences in the meeting(s).
		Prepare the focus student to ask questions or use cues to signal a question during sampling experiences.	Have the student in a position of leadership (e.g., start the meeting, signal topic changes) during the meeting.

the focus student's preferences drive the planning process, having a clear and fluid picture of what is important to him or her is a prerequisite to planning long-term outcomes. When gathering information that will provide a fluid and comprehensive picture of the focus student, consider the student's (a) values and beliefs, (b) interests and preferences, (c) natural and paid supports, and (d) expertise and abilities. We use the acronym VINE as a way of reminding ourselves that these facets of individuals are interwoven throughout their lives and must be considered during all aspects of transition planning, including designing the preference assessment.

Values and beliefs refer to spiritual, emotional, and character creeds that the focus student holds as important. The team may have to interpret the actions of some students as a way of understanding these values or beliefs. For example, do they attend religious services regularly? Are they helpful, respectful, enjoy a good sense of humor, or consider others' feelings? By interpreting their actions, it is possible to identify those values and beliefs important to the student. A second facet to consider is the focus student's currently known interests and preferences. Here, the team may generate lists of things the student likes to do or choices he or she frequently makes. In doing this, the team begins to articulate the individual's current lifestyle preferences. The third facet to consider is the identification of the natural (e.g., friends and family) and paid (e.g., teachers, agency personnel) individuals who can provide various aspects of support, friendship, and companionship both during the transition process and once the student has moved beyond school life. Finally, the team must consider the student's own expertise and skill abilities as he or she plans for the future. All of this information combined creates a rich and descriptive profile of the student that drives the creation of a long-term vision.

Initial Vision Planning

Only after the team has given thoughtful consideration to what they know about the focus student can they begin planning a vision for the future. Planning a vision is a second common element frequently discussed in the person-centered planning and transition-planning literature (e.g., Everson, 1996; Hanley-Maxwell, Whitney-Thomas, & Mayfield Pogoloff, 1995; Malette et al., 1992; Miner & Bates, 1997; Whitney-Thomas, Shaw, Honey, & Butterworth, 1998). Using the information described in VINE, the team begins to generate potential opportunities for the focus student to sample the various lifestyle options available. Table 2 provides examples of characteristics associated with planning decisions in each of the four domain areas. The premise here is that assessing lifestyle preferences is a multistep process that builds on initial information obtained. When deciding on a place to live, for example, the team would begin by considering the individual's preferences for a neighborhood. They might consider variables such as the composition, accessibility to community resources, and the physical appearance. Once a neighborhood is selected, the next task is to define the type of living arrangement the individual desires (e.g., living alone, paid roommate, or living with friends), followed by selecting houses or apartments for the individual to look at considering a diverse range of housing options (e.g., apartment vs. house, multilevel, or living on the first or upper floors). As the team progresses through the assessment, each piece of new information is added to the existing information to guide a final decision. Layering the assessment in this manner allows for

TABLE 2

Characteristics of Lifestyle Planning Decisions and Examples of Assessment Strategies

	Domain		
Living	*Playing*	*Working*	*Learning*
Characteristics of the neighborhood	Types of activities	Field of employment	Types of learning forums
Composition (e.g., young growing families, ethnic diversity, business vs. residential, transient vs. long-term residents)	Scheduled and ongoing (e.g., clubs)	Clerical	College classes
Physical appearance (e.g., cleanliness, greenery)	Spontaneous (e.g., walk through the park)	Food services	Seminars
Accessibility of preferred community resources (e.g., churches, convenience stores, doctors)	Hit and run (e.g., movies)	Landscaping	Workshops and conferences
Type of living arrangement	Home versus community	Specific job tasks	Types of learning experiences
Paid support	Characteristics of activities	Dishwashing	Didactic
Family members	Activity level (e.g., amount of effort)	Filing	Interactional
Friends or same-age peers	Activity participation (e.g., level of involvement required)	Vacuuming	Hands-on
Housing structure	Structure (e.g., rule based, unstructured)	Environmental considerations	Areas of learning
	Planning requirements	Noise level	Business and professional development
Type of housing (e.g., apartment or house)			
Level (e.g., first vs. upper floors)	Cost	Required pace	Personal growth
Amenities (e.g., dishwasher, walk-in shower to accommodate shower chair)	Social dimensions	Indoors versus outdoors	Special interest
Maintenance (e.g., day-to-day repairs, cyclical repairs, general cleaning)	Activity partners	Sitting versus standing	Literacy and adult basic education
	Level of interaction		

the flexibility of adding or eliminating options based on how well they match the focus student's criteria of what is wanted. Because decisions such as where to live and work are so complex, it is necessary to break the assessment into natural segments (e.g., assess neighborhood preferences, then type of living arrangement, then physical structure) that logically build on one another to arrive at a final decision. This way, the student has the opportunity to sample discrete aspects of the planning decision without unnecessarily splintering the sampling experiences from the natural context.

Conduct a Systematic Assessment

Thus far we have described two critical features leading up to conducting the preference assessment. First, the team gathered information using VINE as a format to develop a rich and descriptive profile. Next, the team described an initial vision of long-term postschool outcomes while generating a list of possible lifestyle options for the individual to sample. One concern with nominating lifestyle options through person-centered planning meetings is the extent to which third-party opinion yields accurate information about the student's preferences (Hughes, Middleton, & Green, 2000; Reid, Everson, & Green, 1999). For example, Hughes et al. and Reid et al. used approach and avoidance responses to evaluate the accuracy of leisure options nominated through person-centered planning meetings. These researchers found that only a portion of the options nominated were observed as preferred, and some options were even considered nonpreferred. Nomination of lifestyle options may be even more difficult, especially when the individual relies on nonsymbolic or limited symbolic communication systems. Therefore, this step is for the team to conduct an assessment that provides the focus student with the opportunity to sample nominated lifestyle options. The team begins the assessment by creating a sampling schedule considering the nature of the options being sampled, its potential availability for sampling, and the student's preferences for when to go.

For some sampling opportunities, the team may need to create nontraditional sampling experiences that require brainstorming and problem solving. Consider finding a place to live. Walking around the neighborhood and looking at apartments will provide information about the location, but it does not provide the individual with an understanding of what the experience of living alone or with a friend might be like. For this experience, the team needs to brainstorm possible ways the individual could have the experience of living alone within realistic bounds. One example is providing the focus student with the opportunity to spend a weekend at a local hotel that has rooms with efficiency kitchens. Although limited in scope, such an experience can still provide the focus student with a frame of reference for what it would be like to live on his or her own. Brainstorming and problem solving nontraditional sampling experiences offers the focus student an unusual opportunity to sample a fairly abstract experience in a concrete way.

In another example, Foxx, Faw, Taylor, Davis, and Fulia (1993) and Faw, Davis, and Peck (1996) used contrasting pictures (e.g., empty bathroom vs. a bathroom with people in it) presented in a two-item choice format to solicit information about the individual's living preferences. The information obtained during the assessment was used to teach the individuals to solicit information about potential lifestyle preferences when touring group homes. By making characteristics of the lifestyle option concrete (e.g., through pictures, video clips, or objects), the focus student is more likely to understand the possible options and make selections reflective of their true preferences.

Team members next make commitments for how they will contribute to or participate in the assessment process. Commitments from all members are a very important feature of the team planning process. Because transition assessment and planning can be very comprehensive, it may not be feasible for the special education teacher to assume sole responsibility for the many tasks that need to be accomplished. By incorporating the participation of all team members, the focus student will have more opportunities to explore the options available to him or her and benefit from the diverse perspectives offered. Because of the different roles team members play, the type of commitment made may vary as a function of their role or relationship with the focus student. Once commitments are made, the team then generates time lines for completing the various assessment tasks. Depending on the complexity, the assessment may take several months to complete. As such, setting time lines enables the team to move forward at a reasonable pace, but without overwhelming members' commitments or rushing the focus student through the experience.

To ensure accurate interpretation, team members need to consistently recognize the focus student's communicative responses. To achieve accuracy, define responses that are observable, measurable, and recognizable to all team members. In addition, the definition should include descriptions of preference, nonpreference, and termination responses (e.g., Derby et al., 1995; Koegel, Dyer, & Bell, 1987; Newton, Ard, & Horner, 1993). Hughes et al. (1998) noted that researchers often use collateral responses (e.g., time on task, disruptive behavior) to further corroborate preference (or nonpreference) of the sampling option. The benefit of defining collateral responses when conducting an assessment of lifestyle preferences is that it may not be easy to discern a discrete response to an abstract experience. Rather, considering all of the focus student's responses—including the occurrence of problem behavior, changes in social interactions, facial expressions, and so forth—may provide a more accurate picture of their experience and preference.

A second consideration is the extent that familiarity with the partner or the sampling option affects the responses observed (Nozaki & Mochizuki, 1995). For example, a student sampling an unfamiliar activity may be uncomfortable because of the disruption to his or her routine and subsequently may engage in challenging behaviors. The challenging behaviors may be misinterpreted as an expression of nonpreference when in actuality it was the disruption to routine that triggered the behavior. In addition, the activity partner also may influence a response due to the history (or lack thereof) between the focus student and the partner.

Finalize the Plan

The systematic preference assessment provides the focus student with the opportunity to sample and experience the options available to him or her. Once they have had sufficient exposure to the options available, it is then time to begin finalizing the transition vision. Using those features identified in the assessment for which the focus student expressed a preference, the team begins to build the transition plan specifying the support and skill needs to achieve the desired outcomes. It is at this stage that the team often is faced with barriers (e.g., waiting lists or lack of sufficient funding) and is tasked with having to brainstorm solutions. These barriers could pose such resistance that the team may tire and become susceptible to giving up. However, having clear focus about what is important to the focus student and providing him or her with the opportunity to express those preferences to the team during each meeting will act as a motivator propelling the team forward through planning. In addition, the problem-solving orientation of person-centered planning strengthens the capacity of the team to dismantle barriers encountered (Mount, 1994).

In summary, preference assessment plays a key role in the design of transition plans. To integrate the assessment, the team must build on what they know about the student and offer him or her systematic opportunities to sample various options available. Planning in a team format is a key aspect of using preference assessment within the transition process. The team works together designing and implementing the assessment to solicit the most accurate information possible. The assessment outcomes then are used to finalize a vision for the student that translates into a plan specifying support and skill needs to produce desired outcomes.

SPECIAL CONSIDERATIONS

Because of the complex and abstract nature of lifestyle decisions, applying preference assessment to the transition process may involve several considerations different than assessing day-to-day choices such as food and drink preferences. In light of an absence of empirical direction, the following considerations are offered for integrating preference assessment into the transition process.

Changing Nature of Preferences

For many individuals with significant disabilities and limited communicative ability, determining when preferences change could pose some difficulty. One indicator perhaps could be the occurrence of persistent challenging behaviors that is often symptomatic of dissatisfaction with one's current lifestyle (e.g., Berkman & Meyer, 1988; Lucyshyn, Olson, & Horner, 1995). Another indicator may be the changing circumstances surrounding the individual. When preferred variables in the individual's life are no longer accessible, the individual's preferences also might change. For example, the passing away of a parent might propel the individual to change his or her preference from living in the family's home to living in an apartment independently.

Although research has demonstrated that preferences do change over time, the variability of change is most likely individualized and may be associated with the type or nature of the item or event (e.g., Mason, McGee, Farmer-Dougan, & Risley, 1989). One could assume that lifestyle preferences will change over the course of one's life. These changes, however, are less likely to occur as frequently as some day-to-day choices (e.g., music preferences). The choices we make in our early 20s are typically different from those of our 30s and 40s. Similarly, it is likely that lifestyle preferences expressed at age 14, when specifying the initial transition curriculum, may be different or evolve by the time the student reaches 16, when a formal plan needs to be in place, and again at 21, when it is time to move beyond school life. As such, there is a need for ongoing assessment that captures these changes.

Incorporating the Individual's Participation

To fully promote the community inclusion of students transitioning from school to life, it is critical to provide opportunities for choice and control to make such important decisions (Racino, 1995). Moving into an apartment or getting a job may not produce desired outcomes if these situations do not reflect the preferences and interests of the focus person. To encourage the full and self-determining participation of the focus student, transition teams need to incorporate the student's participation to the greatest extent possible. Promoting self-determination is discussed as an important component of the transition process as well as a desirable outcome (Martin & Huber-Marshall, 1995; Martin, Huber-Marshall, & Maxson, 1993). A complex construct, self-determination, is interactional and relies on both the individual's internal motivation and skill abilities (Bambara, Cole, & Koger, 1998; Wehmeyer, 1998). Further complicating self-determination is the extent that the environment is responsive and supportive of attempts made (Deci, Eghrari, Patrick, & Leone, 1994; Wehmeyer, 1998). In the absence of understanding preference, it is possible to interpret inaccurately what the individual wants even when people supporting the individual have the best of intentions (Bambara et al., 1998). To increase participation and reduce inaccuracies, team members need to consider strategies that will promote the student's participation before, during, and after the preference assessment.

Prior to the assessment, the student can participate in designing a schedule and selecting partners to accompany him or her during sampling opportunities. Using a personalized scheduled (e.g., Bambara & Ager, 1992; Brown, 1991), team members can provide the focus student with choices about when and with whom to go. Using pictures, objects, or words, the schedule is constructed organizing all the information in a format the focus student understands. Team members also can prepare the student in advance with questions to ask about features of the sampling option that are important to him or her (e.g., Faw et al., 1996; Foxx et al., 1993). If the student is nonverbal, pictures or objects can be presented to the community member that signal the sampling partner to ask a question about a particular feature. Part of the goal would be to sufficiently prepare the student so that the sampling partner only speaks on the student's behalf when prompted by the student. This allows the sampling partner to act as a liaison, translating the meaning of the picture while directing all interactions to the focus student.

To increase active participation during sampling opportunities, defer to the student by using respectful interaction behaviors such as speaking directly to the student (e.g., "John, did you want to ask if there are two bathrooms?" vs. "John wants two bathrooms") and making eye contact (Whitney-Thomas et al., 1998). In doing this, the sampling partner models to the community member that the student is the person making the final decision and that all information and interactions should be directed at him or her. Another important way to include students during the assessment process is to listen carefully to their behaviors. Changes in disposition, interactions, or other changes in behavior may signal dissatisfaction or a need to terminate sampling for that day. By interpreting behaviors and honoring their meaning, the sampling partner provides the student with more control over the assessment process.

Once the assessment is completed, the next step is to provide the student with the tools needed to express those preferences within planning meetings. Whitney-Thomas et al. (1998) found that students were more likely to participate actively in planning meetings when team members matched their interactions to the student's conversational style. In addition, these researchers found that students were more likely to participate when a clear pattern of communication was established between the student and the facilitator. Their findings indicated that the facilitator needs to incorporate strategies such as speaking directly to the student, providing the student with time to think, verifying meaning and understanding, and using various accommodations to encourage and maintain active student participation in the planning process.

It may be helpful to assist the focus student to summarize the information obtained in the assessment into a format that they can understand (e.g., videos, pictures, objects, or voice recorders). Because many students may be unable to articulate their preferences, having a concrete tool, such as a picture profile, will encourage their active participation during planning meetings. Koger and Bambara (1995) used picture booklets with two adults that guided them through their planning meetings. The booklets contained picture prompts and were organized according to the beginning, middle, and end of the meeting. A similar strategy could be used during the transition meeting with the booklets containing pictures of the student's lifestyle preferences and long-term goals.

Another way to promote the student's active participation is by having the facilitator and student co-lead the planning meeting together (Browder & Lohrmann-O'Rourke, 2001). For example, having the student call the meeting to order, begin introductions, and signal topic changes in conversation are all roles the student can fulfill (Martin, Huber-Marshall, Maxson, & Jerman, 1996). In taking on these roles, team members are reminded constantly of the focus student's position of leadership within the planning process.

Family and Cultural Issues

When conducting a preference assessment, members of the family need to be involved (Browder, 1991). Not only are family members significant to the focus student, but they also know the individual better than anybody else. Involving the family in the preference assessment requires that the team takes into consideration the family's dynamics and cultural values. First, the team needs to get to know the family well and establish a working relationship with them (Bambara & Browder, 1991). In doing this, the team could become more sensitive to certain family dynamics that could affect the focus student's preferences. Benson and Turnbull (1986) described the family as a system wherein each member is unique and interrelated with the others. This interrelation is manifested in four aspects: (a) family resources (e.g., collective input of the family, number of members, and special knowledge and talents), (b) family interaction (relationships among family members), (c) family functions (various tasks or outputs such as providing economic security, educational guidance, health care, etc. to the family), and (d) family life cycle (significant changes that the family goes through across time such as birth, death, and loss of a job).

These dynamics could affect the family's support for the individual's effort to establish preferences. For example, parents undergoing significant changes such as a divorce (family cycle) could withdraw from participating in their child's assessment process to tend to the demands of the divorce procedures; parents may be unable to take their child to sample potential recreational activities due to a lack of transportation (lack of resources). It is also possible that the preference indicated by the focus student may not be feasible within the family's established routines (family functions). In short, by taking into consideration certain family dynamics, the team could be better prepared for unexpected fluctuations in family support of the focus student.

Second, the team needs to be aware of the family's cultural values. Culture is a fluid term and, in its broadest sense, could refer to any type of diversity such as one's ethnicity, religious beliefs, ideological beliefs, sex, and sexual orientation. Basic to becoming aware of a family's cultural values is the team's awareness of its own cultural values and biases. According to Lim and Browder (1994), "the professional who is not aware of his or her own values [cultural] may not be aware that not all families share these values" (p. 132). Consequently, this could lead to the team's misinterpreting certain family dynamics or being judgmental about the family's actuations. Language is a commonly held issue in assessment of non–English-speaking students (Obiakor, 1999). In planning with families whose first language is not English, the assessment most likely will be facilitated through the use of an independent interpreter (Harry et al., 1995). An additional challenge in working with families from diverse cultures is understanding the nuances of the culture itself as enacted by the family members. This may be particularly difficult when planning occurs through an interpreter. Certain meanings or intentions may be lost when translated out of the family's native language and inadvertently misunderstood by school or community members. Third, given that the family is a dynamic system that is continually in flux, the team needs to adopt a flexible stance when dealing with family members to accommodate numerous family changes.

Interacting With the Community

Parallel to conducting an assessment of preferences is an assessment of the targeted community. Underlying both assessments is finding a match between the individual's preferences and the characteristics of the community that will receive the individual. The first consideration is knowing elements in the community that will facilitate acceptance. Bogdan (1995) found from narratives of participants that certain community variables facilitate acceptance rather than tolerance of individuals with disabilities. These community variables are shared values, being closely knit, being natives of the place, honesty, and contribution of the individual with disabilities. In finding a match between the individual and the community, the team could explore the prevailing values of the community by interviewing key people or spending time to observe a typical routine of the people in the targeted community setting. For example, an observed prevailing value of the community is the value of hard work. Team members could assess the focus student's preference for working hard or degree of self-reliance (e.g., not accepting charity from others). Another community value is the pride that people take in the achievements of others in the community. Team members could assess possible contributions that the focus student could give.

A second consideration is making and maintaining connections with people in the community. Establishing ongoing communication with community members is essential to support the individual's preferences. An initial step would be to involve members from targeted community environments such as work, a recreational facility, neighbors, and others who potentially could support the focus student in the transition planning. Unfortunately, these community members often are excluded from the planning process (Morgan et al., 1992). An advantage to maintaining connections with community members is the ongoing input they could provide the team regarding community requirements. Local employers, for example, routinely could update the team on not only job opportunities, but also the changing demands of the employment market. Such input could guide the team in their assessment of the focus student as well as expand their range of preferences. Maintaining ongoing communication with community members also is seen as a potential benefit to the team in that it promotes a sense of empowerment among community members and enables them to assume certain roles in supporting the focus student as he or she leaves school.

The Emerging Role of Professionals

A special education teacher typically is perceived as the person responsible for transition planning (Morgan et al., 1992) and is charged with coordinating and using assessment information in the decision-making and planning processes. By utilizing a person-centered planning approach, the role of the special education teacher expands to include that of being a group facilitator. This role requires that the special education teacher become sensitive to the group dynamics and have a keen sense of discerning and listening skills. As a facilitator, the teacher uses certain communication leads such as clarification, interpretation, probing questions, and explanations to ensure that preferences of the individual are translated accurately to the group or that ideas from each team member are well understood by the focus student. Depending on the personality of the special education teacher and the team climate, facilitation could be either directive or nondirective. Outside of the transition-planning meeting, the role of the facilitator is expanded further to include establishing connections with the community. In addition to the role of being a facilitator, a special education teacher also could serve as a model for the focus student and his or her family. More specifically, the teacher models the various tasks and responsibilities that are inherent in a longitudinal planning process with the intent that family members or the focus student ultimately will assume those responsibilities.

SUMMARY AND FUTURE RESEARCH DIRECTIONS

Transition planning, person-centered planning, and preference assessment are compatible processes that, when used together, have the ability to produce long-term goals that are reflective of the focus student's desired lifestyle. This discussion built on existing works in the area of person-centered planning and preference assessment to illustrate the use of a team planning format for using preference assessment as a vehicle for designing a transition plan. Future research in this area will need to address several pertinent issues to move the field forward. First, thus far, the research on preference assessment has not to any great extent produced examples of how to design assessments to capture complex and abstract lifestyle decisions such as finding a home or a job (e.g., Winking, O'Reilly, & Moon, 1993). Transition teams are in need of clear, empirically based guidelines illustrating a methodology for conducting such a broad scale assessment. Second, there is no clear guidance regarding the nature of changing lifestyle preferences, the potential indicators of change, or the parameters to capture these changes. Future research will need to explore the frequency, variability, and potential indicators of changes in lifestyle preference to provide guidance regarding the parameters associated with ongoing assessment of major life decisions. Third, future research will need to investigate issues of participation that (a) increase the involvement of the focus student, (b) are reflective of the family's cultural nuances, (c) involve the community to a greater extent, and (d) capture the facilitation skills needed by the special education teacher to effectively orchestrate the planning process, taking into consideration the aforementioned participation needs.

REFERENCES

Baer, R., Simmons, T., & Flexer, R. (1996). Transition practice and policy compliance in Ohio: A survey of secondary educators. *Career Development for Exceptional Individuals, 19*, 61–77.

Bambara, L. M., & Ager, C. (1992). Using self-scheduling to promote self-directed leisure activity in home and community settings. *The Journal of the Association for Persons With Severe Handicaps, 17*, 67–76.

Bambara, L. M., & Browder, D. M. (1991). Assessment in and for the home. In D. M. Browder (Ed.), *Assessment of individuals with severe disabilities: An applied behavior approach to life skills assessment* (2nd ed., pp. 137–212). Baltimore: Brookes.

Bambara, L. M., Cole, C. L., & Koger, F. (1998). Translating self-determination concepts into support for adults with severe disabilities. *The Journal of the Association for Persons With Severe Handicaps, 23*, 27–37.

Benson, H. A., & Turnbull, A. P. (1986). Approach families from an individualized perspective. In R. H. Horner, L. H. Meyer, & H. D. B. Fredericks (Eds.), *Education of learners with severe handicaps: Exemplary service strategies* (pp. 127–157). Baltimore: Brookes.

Berkman, K. A., & Meyer, L. H. (1988). Alternative strategies and multiple outcomes in the remediation of severe self-injury: Going "all out" nonaversively. *The Journal of the Association for Persons With Severe Handicaps, 13*, 76–86.

Blackorby, J., & Wagner, M. (1996). Longitudinal postschool outcomes of youth with disabilities: Findings from the national longitudinal transition study. *Exceptional Children, 62*, 399–413.

Bogdan, R. (1995). A "simple" farmer accused of murder: The case of Delbert Ward. In S. J. Taylor, R. Bogdan, & Z. M. Lutfiyya (Eds.), *The variety of community experience: Qualitative studies of family and community life* (pp. 79–99). Baltimore: Brookes.

Browder, D. M. (1991). *Assessment of individuals with severe disabilities: An applied behavior approach to life skills assessment.* Baltimore: Brookes.

Browder, D. M., & Lohrmann-O'Rourke, S. (2001). Promoting self-determination in planning and instruction. In D. M. Browder (Ed.), *Life skills instruction* (pp. 148–178). New York: Guilford.

Brown, F. (1991). Creative daily scheduling: A nonintrusive approach to challenging behaviors in community residents. *The Journal of the Association for Persons With Severe Handicaps, 16*, 75–84.

Brown, F., Gothelf, C. R., Guess, D., & Lehr, D. H. (1998). Self-determination for individuals with the most severe disabilities: Moving beyond chimera. *The Journal of the Association for Persons With Severe Handicaps, 23*, 17–26.

Butterfield, N., & Arthur, M. (1995). Shifting the focus: Emerging priorities in communication programming for students with a severe intellectual disability. *Education and Training in Mental Retardation and Developmental Disabilities, 30*, 41–50.

Butterworth, J., Hagner, D., Heikkinen, B., Faris, D., DeMello, S., & McDonough, K. (1993). *Whole life planning: A guide for organizers and facilitators.* Boston: Institute for Community Inclusion, Children's Hospital.

Deci, E. L., Eghrari, H., Patrick, B. C., & Leone, D. R. (1994). Facilitating internalization: The self-determination theory perspective. *Journal of Personality, 62*, 119–141.

deFur, S., Getzel, E. E., & Kregel, J. (1994). Individual transition plans: A work in progress. *Journal of Vocational Rehabilitation, 4*, 139–145.

Derby, K. M., Wacker, D. P., Andelman, M., Berg, W., Drew, J., Asmus, J., Prouty, A. M., & Laffey, P. (1995). Two measures of preference during forced-choice assessments. *Journal of Applied Behavior Analysis, 28,* 345–346.

Dyer, K. (1987). The competition of autistic stereotyped behavior with usual and specially assessed reinforcers. *Research in Developmental Disabilities, 8,* 607–626.

Everson, J. (1996). Using person-centered planning concepts to enhance school-to-adult life transition planning. *Journal of Vocational Rehabilitation, 6,* 7–13.

Faw, G. E., Davis, P. K., & Peck, C. (1996). Increasing self-determination: Teaching people with mental retardation to evaluate residential options. *Journal of Applied Behavior Analysis, 29,* 173–188.

Field, S., & Hoffman, A. (1994). Development of a model for self-determination. *Career Development for Exceptional Learners, 17,* 159–169.

Foxx, R. M., Faw, G. D., Taylor, S., Davis, P. K., & Fulia, R. (1993). "Would I be able to …?" Teaching clients to assess the availability of their community living life style preferences. *American Journal on Mental Retardation, 98,* 235–248.

Furney, K. S., Hasazi, S. B., & De Stefano, L. (1997). Transition policies, practices, and promises: Lessons from three states. *Exceptional Children, 63,* 343–355.

Grigal, M., Test, D. W., Beattie, J., & Wood, W. M. (1997). An evaluation of transition components of individualized education programs. *Exceptional Children, 63,* 357–372.

Hagner, J., Helm, D., & Butterworth, J. (1996). "This is our meeting": A qualitative study of person-centered planning. *Mental Retardation, 34,* 159–171.

Hanley-Maxwell, C., Whitney-Thomas, J., & Mayfield Pogoloff, S. (1995). The second shock: A qualitative study of parents' perspectives and needs during their child's transition from school to adult life. *The Journal of the Association for Persons With Severe Handicaps, 20,* 3–15.

Harry, B., Grenot-Scheyer, M., Smith-Lewis, M., Park, H. P., Xin, F., & Schwartz, I. (1995). Developing culturally inclusive services for individuals with severe disabilities. *The Journal of the Association for Persons With Severe Handicaps, 20,* 99–109.

Hughes, C., Eisenman, L. T., Hwang, B., Kim, J. H., Killian, D. J., & Scott, S. V. (1997). Transition from secondary special education to adult life: A review and analysis of empirical measures. *Education and Training in Mental Retardation and Developmental Disabilities, 32,* 85–104.

Hughes, C. W., Middleton, S. G., & Reid, D. H. (2000). Embedded evaluation of preferences sampled from person-centered plans for people with profound multiple disabilities. *Journal of Applied Behavior Analysis, 33,* 639–642.

Hughes, C., Pitkin, S. E., & Lorden, S. W. (1998). Assessing preferences and choices of persons with severe and profound mental retardation. *Education and Training in Mental Retardation and Developmental Disabilities, 33,* 299–316.

Koegel, R. L., Dyer, K., & Bell, L. K. (1987). The influence of child preferred activities on autistic children's social behavior. *Journal of Applied Behavior Analysis, 20,* 243–252.

Koger, F., & Bambara, L. M. (1995, December). *Teaching adults to direct their own planning meeting.* Paper presented at the 21st annual convention of the Association for Applied Behavior Analysis, Washington, DC.

Lichtenstein, S. (1993). Transition from school to adulthood: Case studies of adults with learning disabilities who dropped out of school. *Exceptional Children, 59,* 336–347.

Lichtenstein, S., & Michaelides, N. (1993). Transition from school to adulthood: Four case studies of young adults labeled mentally retarded. *Career Development for Exceptional Individuals, 16,* 183–195.

Lim, L., & Browder, D. M. (1994). Multicultural life skills assessment of individuals with severe disabilities. *The Journal of the Association for Persons With Severe Handicaps, 19,* 130–138.

Lohrmann-O'Rourke, S., & Browder, D. M. (1998). Empirically based methods to assess the preferences of individuals with severe disabilities. *American Journal on Mental Retardation, 103,* 146–161.

Lohrmann-O'Rourke, S., Browder, D. M., & Brown, F. (2000). Guidelines for conducting socially valid systematic preference assessments. *The Journal of the Association for Persons With Severe Handicaps, 25,* 42–53.

Lucyshyn, J. M., Olson, D., & Horner, R. H. (1995). Building an ecology of support: A case study of one young woman with severe problem behaviors living in the community. *The Journal of the Association for Persons With Severe Handicaps, 20,* 16–30.

Malette, P., Mirenda, P., Kandborg, T., Jones, P., Bunz, T., & Rogow, S. (1992). Application of a lifestyle development process for persons with severe intellectual disabilities: A case study report. *The Journal of the Association for Persons With Severe Handicaps, 17,* 179–191.

Martin, J. E., & Huber-Marshall, L. (1995). Choicemaker: A comprehensive self-determination transition program. *Intervention in School and Clinic, 30,* 147–156.

Martin, J. E., Huber-Marshall, L., & Maxson, L. L. (1993). Transition policy: Infusing self-determination and self-advocacy into transition programs. *Career Development for Exceptional Individuals, 16,* 53–61.

Martin, J. E., Huber-Marshall, L., Maxson, L. L., & Jerman, P. (1996). *Self-directed IEP.* Longmont, CO: Sopris West.

Mason, S. A., McGee, G. G., Farmer-Dougan, V., & Risley, T. R. (1989). A practical strategy for ongoing reinforcer assessment. *Journal of Applied Behavior Analysis, 22,* 171–179.

Miner, C. A., & Bates, P. E. (1997). The effect of person centered activities on the IEP/transition planning process. *Education and Training in Mental Retardation and Developmental Disabilities, 32,* 105–112.

Morgan, R. L., Moore, S. C., McSweyn, C., & Salzberg, C. L. (1992). Transition from school to work: Views of secondary special educators. *Education and Training in Mental Retardation, 27,* 315–323.

Mount, B. (1994). Benefits and limitations of personal futures planning. In V. J. Bradley, J. W. Ashbaugh, & B. C. Blaney (Eds.), *Creating individual supports for people with developmental disabilities: A mandate for change at many levels* (pp. 97–108). Baltimore: Brookes.

Mount, B., & Zwernick, K. (1988). *It's never too early. It's never too late. A booklet about personal futures planning for persons with developmental disabilities, their families and friends, case managers, service providers, and advocates.* St. Paul, MN: Metropolitan Council.

Newton, J. S., Ard, W. R., & Horner, R. H. (1993). Validating predicted activity preferences of individuals with severe disabilities. *Journal of Applied Behavior Analysis, 26,* 239–245.

Newton, J. S., Horner, R. H., & Lund, L. (1991). Honoring activity preferences in individualized plan development: A descriptive analysis. *The Journal of the Association for Persons With Severe Handicaps, 16,* 207–212.

Nozaki, K., & Mochizuki, A. (1995). Assessing choice making of a person with profound disabilities: A preliminary analysis. *The Journal of the Association for Persons With Severe Handicaps, 20,* 196–201.

Obiakor, F. E. (1999). Teacher expectations of minority exceptional learners: Impact on "accuracy" of self-concepts. *Exceptional Children, 66,* 39–53.

O'Brien, J. (1987). A guide to life-style planning. In B. Wilcox & G. T. Bellamy (Eds.), *A comprehensive guide to the activities catalog: An alternative curriculum for youth and adults with severe disabilities* (pp. 175–189). Baltimore: Brookes.

Racino, J. A. (1995). Community living for adults with developmental disabilities: A housing and support approach. *The Journal of the Association for Persons With Severe Handicaps, 20,* 300–310.

Reid, D. H., Everson, J. M., & Green, C. W. (1999). A systematic evaluation of preferences identified through person-centered planning for people with profound multiple disabilities. *Journal of Applied Behavior Analysis, 32,* 467–478.

Sitlington, P., Neubert, D., & Leconte, P. (1997). Transition assessment: The position of the division on career development and transition. *Career Development for Exceptional Individuals, 20,* 69–79.

Taylor, S. J., & Bogdan, R. (1989). On accepting relationships between people with mental retardation and non-disabled people: Towards and understanding of acceptance. *Disability, Handicap, & Society, 4,* 21–36.

Walker, P. (1999). From community presence to sense of place: Community experiences of adults with developmental disabilities. *The Journal of the Association for Persons With Severe Disabilities, 24,* 23–32.

Wehmeyer, M. L. (1998). Self-determination and individuals with significant disabilities: Examining meanings and misinterpretations. *The Journal of the Association for Persons With Severe Handicaps, 23,* 5–16.

Wehmeyer, M. L., & Lawrence, M. (1995). Whose future is it anyway? Promoting student involvement in transition planning. *Career Development for Exceptional Individuals, 18,* 69–83.

Wehmeyer, M. L., & Schwartz, M. (1998). The self-determination focus of transition goals for students with mental retardation. *Career Development for Exceptional Individuals, 21,* 75–86.

Whitney-Thomas, J., Shaw, D., Honey, K., & Butterworth, J. (1998). Building a future: A study of student participation in person-centered planning. *The Journal of the Association for Persons With Severe Handicaps, 23,* 119–133.

Winking, D. L., O'Reilly, B., & Moon, M. S. (1993). Preference: The missing link in the job match process for individuals without functional communication skills. *Journal of Vocational Rehabilitation, 3,* 27–42.